THE AFFECTIVE Curriculum

TEACHING THE ANTI-BIAS APPROACH TO YOUNG CHILDREN

NADIA SADERMAN HALL

VALERIE RHOMBERG

Nelson Canada

I(T)P An International Thomson Publishing Company

Toronto • Albany • Bonn • Boston • Cincinnati • Detroit • London • Madrid • Melbourne
Mexico City • New York • Pacific Grove • Paris • San Francisco • Singapore • Tokyo • Washington

I(T)P™
International Thomson Publishing
The ITP logo is a trademark under licence

Published in 1995 by
Nelson Canada
A division of Thomson Canada Limited
1120 Birchmount Road, Scarborough, Ontario M1K 5G4

Cover illustration: Stéphan Daigle
Page formatting: New Concept Complete Printing & Publishing Services Ltd.

Canadian Cataloguing in Publication Data

Hall, Nadia Saderman, 1952–
   The affective curriculum : teaching the anti-bias approach to young children

Includes bibliographical references and index.
ISBN 0-17-604858-8

1. Early childhood education – Curricula.
2. Prejudices – Study and teaching (Preschool).
3. Social values – Study and teaching (Preschool).
4. Discrimination in education 5. Early childhood education – Activity programs.   I. Rhomberg, Valerie, date.   II. Title.

LB1139.4H35 1995   372.13   C94-932312-9

Acquisitions Editor	Charlotte Forbes
Production Editor	Bob Kohlmeier
Developmental Editor	Heather Martin
Art Director	Liz Harasymczuk
Design	Katharine Lapins
Graphic Communications Manager	Deborah Woodman
Senior Production Coordinator	Sheryl Emery
Input Operator	Michelle Volk

Printed and bound in Canada
1 2 3 4 (BG) 98 97 96 95

*This book is dedicated
to our mothers,
who have lived the anti-bias approach
all their lives.*

Contents

Preface

The origins of this book date from 1989, when Louise Derman-Sparks presented her "Anti-Bias Curriculum" workshop at the National Association for the Education of Young Children Conference (NAEYC). The ideas were inspiring and when we returned to Canada we made every attempt to integrate the key concepts in the Early Childhood Education diploma program at Canadian Mothercraft. It soon became apparent that this topic needed a more comprehensive examination.

Initially, early childhood practitioners put up much resistance to the term "anti-bias": they felt we were stirring up feelings of discrimination. But by 1993 early childhood practitioners were expressing a great deal of interest in the topic and the authors developed a full course on anti-bias education. At the same time, the Municipality of Metropolitan Toronto launched a forum exploring racism in the child-care system. Since then, the Children's Services Division of Toronto has sponsored many training events on this issue, while on the provincial level a commitment to combatting racism in the workplace has resulted in the mandatory adoption of an anti-racist policy by funded agencies in Ontario.

During our workshops and training sessions, we were met with frequent requests for a book that specifically dealt with designing and implementing activities that promoted the anti-bias philosophy. Although a recipe-type activity book was demanded, we did not feel comfortable with this format alone. This text endeavours to help those working with children to think critically about the reasons for an activity and how it fits into the larger framework of anti-bias education. This text represents four years of listening to students, ECE practitioners, supervisors of child-care centres, parents, and government program advisors. We have attempted to meet all of these various needs.

For trainers—who must bear the responsibility of teaching new educators how to evaluate programs, design curricula, and implement teaching strategies—this text assists prospective teachers to explore how their personal values and attitudes influence what they choose to do with children, and how they do it.

For supervisors, the text offers opportunities for professional development with staff. Staff can begin to evaluate program effectiveness in responding to larger social issues as well as considering the dimension of family involvement.

For the early childhood practitioner, the book attempts to clarify their understanding of children's developmental abilities in relation to diversity. It offers clear guidelines on broader program goals and specific developmental skills that children need to practise in order to acquire the skills necessary for living sensitively in a world of diversity.

For students, the text attempts to familiarize them with all the key dimensions involved in creating a responsive atmosphere for young children's growth; this includes program development, arrangement of the physical environment, and the critical component of social interaction.

For families, this text provides information on how quality programs should function. In addition, families will gain ideas about experiences they can share with their own children.

We recognize that this text cannot be everything to all readers. We admit that the topic of working with families has not been specifically addressed. We have, however, attempted to weave the broad definition of family into the activity designs and their implementation. We fully acknowledge that *who* a child is and *who* that child will become is vitally linked to the child's perception of self in relation to his or her family.

It is our hope that this text bridges the gap that exists between child-development texts and curriculum resources by offering suggestions on how to apply recent research in a creative way. This text will be of optimal benefit if used in conjunction with a curriculum/methodology course. Our overriding consideration in designing the activities was that their implementation *never* be forced, but that they be presented in a natural, integrated manner. Finally, a note about political correctness. Terms that are politically correct today may not be politically correct tomorrow, so authors who use them must accept their changeable nature. The terms we use in this text received a positive response at every stage in the manuscript review process, but if over time those same terms fall into disfavour, we hope that our readers remember the spirit of the times in which the text was written.

ACKNOWLEDGMENTS

This text would never have come to be without key players in our lives. Our professional growth could not have occurred without the ongoing support of the Canadian Mothercraft Society of Toronto. The administration and the faculty always offered us constructive feedback and kept us on track. The Mothercraft ECE students from 1990 to 1994 challenged us and yet demonstrated a creativity that inspired us. For that, we owe them a great deal of gratitude. Workshop participants challenged us from a practitioner's perspective and enabled us to focus on how to best meet their needs. The Association of Early Childhood Educators' Provincial (Ontario) Week of the Child Committee provided our first opportunity to present an anti-bias workshop in 1990. We are grateful for the risk they took.

To our colleagues Carol Goldman and Pearl Rimer, we are indebted for their critical appraisal and editing suggestions of the initial draft. We are grateful also for the comments and suggestions on the manuscript that were provided by our peers in other schools and facilities: Carol Goldman, Cresthaven Preschool; Sue Hunter, Metro Community Services, Children's Services Division (Toronto); Leslie Kopf-Johnson, Algonquin College; Allison Soave, Niagara College; Alice Taylor, Holland College; and Goranka Vukelich, Mohawk College.

To Angelique Davies and Dina Hill, we owe our sincere thanks for their tireless legwork in researching the section on Canadian resources. We would like to thank the children and staff of Kensington, Montrose, and Rosalie Hall child-care centres for the privilege of photographing them.

We would also like to thank our children for keeping us aware of the causes that make self-esteem so vulnerable. To Rebecca and Alec, you keep me vigilant in instilling pro-activism in your lives. To Regina and Patti, you have demonstrated how empowerment can be used to help others.

Finally, we would like to thank our long-suffering husbands: Michael, who patiently waited for his turn on the computer, and Rudy, without whom the charts in this book would not have been possible.

Nadia Saderman Hall and Valerie Rhomberg
1994

About the Authors

Nadia Saderman Hall has for over seven years managed training programs at the community-college level at Canadian Mothercraft Society. Her primary focus is infant mental health. She has been active in curriculum design and program development, and has developed a post-diploma specialization in infancy for ECE

practitioners; a collaborative project with Native Child and Family Services, Toronto, which created a culturally specific training program focused on prevention and support for children and families in that city's native community; and the Anti-Bias Post-Diploma course developed in response to Metro Toronto's Anti-Racist Education in Child Care Committee.

She has taught curriculum and child development courses for over ten years and has delivered many workshops and addresses all over Canada.

She began her professional career as an infant therapist in a home intervention program, and shortly after created and co-directed the Infant–Parent Learning Program, which helped new parents understand infant developmental issues.

She holds an M.A. from the University of Toronto; an M.Ed. from the Ontario Institute of Education, University of Toronto; a Diploma of Child Study from the Institute of Child Study, University of Toronto; and a Teacher Certificate, Primary Specialist, from the University of Toronto.

Valerie Rhomberg is an early childhood educator and consultant whose teaching experience over the past 20 years has spanned all age groups—infants to adults—in diverse educational settings in Canada and Europe.

She founded and codirected a private Children's Program for the Gifted, directed an infant-to-school-age Toronto-based child-care centre, and taught various age groups in licensed centres and public schools.

She currently holds the position of coordinator in the School of Child and Family Studies at Canadian Mothercraft Society in Toronto; teaches courses at the ECE level; and delivers post-diploma training in anti-bias. She is also the supervisor of the Childcare Learning Centre affiliated with the school. As well, she consults in early childhood-related matters for C.C.E., a Toronto-based educational consulting firm.

Her focus is anti-bias. She attempts to weave this into all aspects of her work. Her numerous articles, workshops, and presentations on anti-bias and other issues—at local, provincial, and national levels—demonstrated a clear need for a course in anti-bias, and with Nadia Hall she developed the Anti-Bias Post-Diploma course.

Her many professionally related volunteer positions include facilitator at Metro Toronto's first race-relations forum, "Towards a New Response"; member of the working committee of the Toronto Bias Free Resource Centre; working member of the National Diversity Network, Canada; and co-chair of the Professional Development Committee of the AECEO. As a parent she was actively involved in the first French immersion program ever offered in Toronto.

Born in Europe, educated at universities in Vienna and Toronto, she is currently working toward a master's degree.

The Child of all Children

A mother reads out to a child that is not hers
She sees that different races don't matter if it is a child in distress
She takes it upon herself to be this child's guardian
The mother doesn't know it, but she is now mothering the child of all children
For this baby is both black, white, brown, and mulato
Muslim, Christian, Jewish, and Catholic
This baby is one and everyone

Rebecca Hall
age 10

CHAPTER 1

An Introduction to the Anti-Bias Approach

PURPOSE

• *To define the foundations of an anti-bias approach to working with young children*
• *To become familiar with the different areas of bias*

STRATEGIES

• *Examination of the steps of responsiveness and empowerment by using the suggested chart*
• *Identification of areas of bias through individual and small-group exercises*

MAKING THE CONNECTION

• *To recognize the attitudes that foster an anti-bias approach*
• *To gain insight into the barriers that hinder the implementation of such an approach*

Anti-Bias: An Introduction

RESPECT, ACCEPTANCE, AND SELF-WORTH

"Everything we do, every decision we make and course of action we take, is based on our consciously or unconsciously held beliefs, attitudes and values" (Simon et al., 1972, 13). This statement is critical to early childhood education. When teachers work with young children and their families, countless interactions and decisions occur. Whether everyone involved will feel respected and accepted largely depends on how the caregivers respond to the families.

At the heart of any interaction with young children is the concern for their well-being. How can this be put into best practice so that feelings of positive **self-identity** and self-worth are promoted? What roles must adults play in the process of developing the full potential of each child?

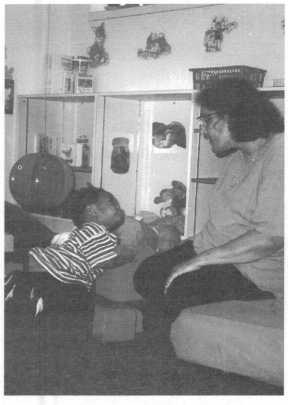

Acceptance and nurturing is the foundation of self-worth.

Definition of Anti-Bias

An **anti-bias** philosophy promotes attitudes of **respect** and **acceptance**, within an inclusionary atmosphere of **diversity**. In order to understand the anti-bias approach, the terms should be defined and the areas in which bias can occur should be clarified.

Bias is a point of view or inclination that manifests itself through favoritism, dislike, or fear toward someone because of that person's particular looks, behaviour, or lifestyle. A bias can be conveyed to another through nonverbal, verbal, and physical interactions. In other words, one's point of view is clearly reflected by one's attitude and actions.

"Anti" means "against." An anti-bias approach, then, means taking a stand against unfair treatment associated with one of the areas of diversity where bias may exist.

AREAS OF BIAS

For the purposes of this book, the following areas are identified and defined:

Ability describes physical, mental, and emotional abilities or a range of any of these. The abilities most commonly recognized by young children are physical in nature.

Age refers to looking or being old or young.

Appearance refers to height (short, tall), size (fat, skinny), and conditions that disfigure, such as scars or burns.

Belief encompasses what a person does or does not believe in. This includes various institutionalized religions, atheism, belief in the power of nature and spiritualism, and political beliefs.

Class (socioeconomic status) indicates the social and economic values that reflect a person's lifestyle. Common elements which determine class are a person's occupation, type of housing, clothing, mode of transportation, and educational background.

Culture is a way of living shared with other members of the same group. This includes ways of thinking, beliefs, language spoken, holidays and celebrations, and customs that reflect integral aspects of behaviour toward others. Each of us belongs to different cultures found within the family, ethnic group, and society.

Family composition refers to the structure of families: who are its members and head of the household, and what role is assigned to individual members.

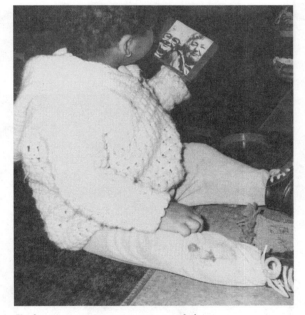

Gender designates a person as male or female; issues around gender commonly deal with roles assigned to or associated with maleness/femaleness. **Discrimination** due to gender is called sexism.

Race refers to a group of people connected by a common origin and a set of physical characteristics that are genetically determined, such as skin colour, hair form, and facial and body appearance. Each race incorporates many ethnic groups.

Early exposure promotes open-mindedness.

Sexuality refers to sexual orientation and preferences. Issues often deal with family composition (gay or lesbian couples) and **homophobia**.

These 10 areas constitute the primary sources of bias. Given the fact that all of us are, to a certain extent, the product of our time and our environment, it is unrealistic to expect individuals to be completely without bias. We will always have preferences, but to act on them in an exclusionary manner constitutes a bias. Attempts at inclusion begin with multiculturalism. (For a short discussion on the difference between multicultural education and anti-bias, anti-racist education, see the Appendix on page 17.)

INCLUSION—BEYOND MULTICULTURALISM

Although multicultural education has been a focus of North American child care for over a decade, the face of diversity has become more complex and multidimensional. Incorporating such diversity moves the education of young children beyond multiculturalism. Adults can nurture feelings of belonging in children through the adoption of inclusionary attitudes. **Inclusion** can be defined as "no one being left out," or "helping everyone to feel a part of" an activity or situation. Modelling positive interactions within an inclusive atmosphere fosters healthy emotions in children.

Teacher training has had to shift its focus from multiculturalism to inclusiveness. This kind of training must examine the areas of diversity that exist within the scope of early childhood experiences. It must investigate bias that may occur in these "areas" and explore reasons for its presence. Finally, it should offer strategies to counteract the bias. This humanistic orientation enables everyone involved in the education of young children to learn the steps necessary for responsiveness and empowerment. (See Diagram 1.1.)

The core of the anti-bias approach builds upon the emotional well-being of children. Planning a curriculum within such a framework of inclusion will naturally result in each child acquiring positive feelings of self.

Responsiveness begins in infancy.

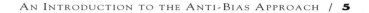

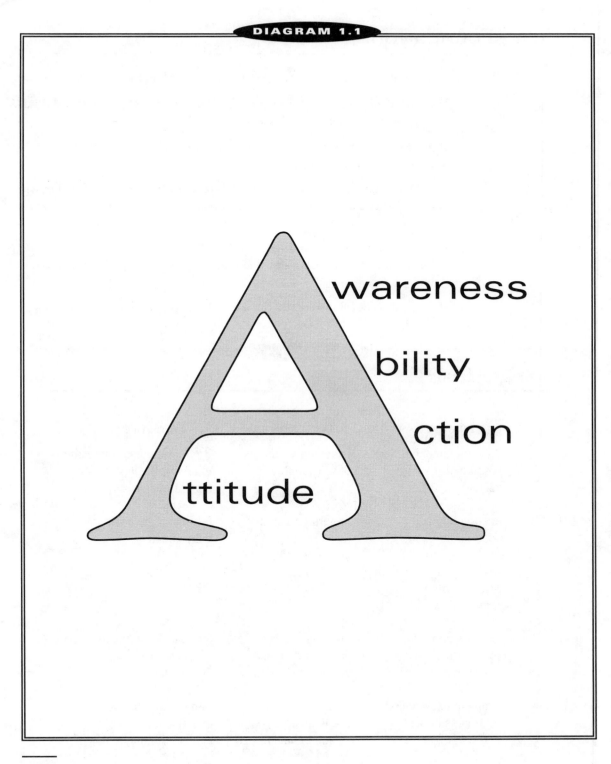

Source: Valerie Rhomberg.

Foundations

According to Louise Derman-Sparks, the anti-bias curriculum has four major goals.

1. To enable children to have a strong sense of self, which helps them to feel good, but not superior, about their self-identity.

2. To enable children to feel comfortable with one another and with differences, which helps them to feel **empathy** for others.

3. To enable children to think critically and seriously about how they and others feel when encountering inequities, which helps them to differentiate between fair and unfair treatment.

4. To enable children to stand up for themselves and for others when facing unfairness and bias, which helps them learn to take action (Derman-Sparks, 1989).

Each of these goals is developmentally linked to the cognitive, language, and affective domains.

CHART 1.1

DEVELOPMENTAL LINK

	COGNITIVE	LANGUAGE	AFFECTIVE
Goal 1	Recognition of gender, physical traits and abilities	Labelling attributes of self-identity	Understanding relationship to family; feeling good about oneself
Goal 2	Recognition and understanding of similarities and differences among people; seeing another point of view	Inquiring respectfully about differences	Feeling at ease with differences
Goal 3	Thinking about fair/unfair or discriminatory acts/words	Identifying fair/unfair or discriminatory actions/words	Showing empathy for feelings that have been hurt due to bias
Goal 4	Taking action against unfairness or bias	Learning how to speak up against biased behaviour	Demonstrating empathy due to an unjust act/comment

THE AFFECTIVE DOMAIN AND THE ANTI-BIAS APPROACH

Emotional well-being is an important part of the healthy development of any child. The affective domain deals with emotions that translate into feelings and dictate behaviour. Feelings have a direct link to children's actions. Helping children feel good about themselves will ultimately give them the ability to behave in ways which make others feel good. This cyclical pattern of behaving thoughtfully toward others builds self-worth and **self-esteem**.

The affective domain influences all other developmental domains. The following anecdote reveals the impact of a negative experience on a child's affective development.

A three-year-old black child who was attending child care had demonstrated pride in his self-identity and had never displayed any discomfort with his skin colour. One day he returned home from child care and began to cry, "Mom, I don't want to be black. I hate being black." He began to exhibit eating and sleeping difficulties and lost his ability to concentrate. His mother became distraught over the radical change in her son's behaviour and emotional state, and turned to the child-care staff for a possible explanation. The staff recounted that one day a story had been read to the children in which the villain was black. There was no discussion after the story. The child, because of his limited thinking skills (developmentally appropriate), interpreted the story in such a way that black was *bad*. Immature reasoning ability led him to conclude that since he was black, he had to be bad, and therefore he did not want to be black.

As this anecdote illustrates, the feelings provoked in children can have a powerful influence on their overall developmental progress. Thus the attainment of the four anti-bias curriculum goals promotes affective development by:

1. Fostering a sense of well-being within each child

2. Centring each child's outlook on others in a humanistic fashion

It follows that affective educational objectives can be met in the context of an anti-bias approach.

ATTITUDES AND BARRIERS

Attitude is the cornerstone on which the foundation of the anti-bias approach rests.

Can attitude become a barrier when attempting to deliver an anti-bias environment? Whether one's attitude turns into a barrier will depend largely on the degree of self-awareness one displays toward the 10 identified areas of bias. Unless vague, unclear, or hostile feelings are examined, addressed, and resolved, they will lead to discomfort. This discomfort may be translated in three ways:

- *Nonverbal*—body language, such as stiffening of the whole body, avoidance of eye contact, inappropriate facial expression
- *Verbal*—language, such as inappropriate jokes, labelling, making abusive comments

Labelling attributes about self-identity.

- *Physical*—actions, such as leaving a room, hitting, pushing, swarming (Rhomberg, 1993–94, *E.C.E. Link* [a])

Creating an Environment That Fosters an Anti-Bias Attitude

Adults play a primary role in the type of atmosphere they promote in their programs. **Realization** by the adults of their own attitudes in relation to the areas of bias is the first step toward creating an environment which fosters inclusion. **Recognition** of these attitudes leads to an understanding of personal values and biases. **Awareness** of these attitudes, and more importantly their origins, prevent the imposition of this negativism on others.

Acknowledgment of biases then enables adults to model appropriate strategies when faced with situations of discrimination or **prejudice**. Thus **realization, recognition, and acknowledgment** are the keys to self-awareness. It is these behaviours that promote the attitudes of respect and acceptance. By following these behaviours, adults become empowered. Empowerment leads to affirmative action and change. In this manner, adults establish a tone and an expectation for children to emulate. Eventually children will learn to respond to bias in the same fashion.

Modelling is a key factor in guiding children's behaviour. Modelling takes place both through **omission** and **commission**. How adults react to situations has a strong influence on the way children will behave when faced with similar experiences. Modelling a **pro-active** approach toward inequities lays a firm foundation for the demonstration of respect toward others. The success of an anti-bias program depends on the degree to which everyone associated with this program embodies the attitude of inclusiveness and respect for diversity. (See Chart 1.2.)

Realization, Recognition, and Acknowledgment

Discomfort with the areas of bias most often stems from fear of the unknown and/or the sincere belief that the way one thinks or acts is best. An examination of society's evolving norms of parenthood serves as a good example.

In the 1950s, the ideal Western family consisted of a working father, an "at home" mother, and children whose needs were met at home and not in child care. Any family structure outside of this norm was viewed negatively.

In the 1980s, child care became an acceptable option as the two-income family became a reality. Over a 30-year period, the norm of family composition was challenged by mothers who held dual job responsibilities, by increasing numbers of divorced families, and by many adults who were exercising the option of single parenthood.

A common scenario in the 1990s is that of a single woman for whom giving birth or adopting a child have become viable options. The decision to raise a child by oneself challenges **values** which many people cherish concerning family structure and the kind of environment in which children thrive.

In such a scenario, an attitude of discomfort may make it difficult to interact in a supportive manner with someone who chooses to act somewhat differently from the norm. In the best possible world, one would need to suspend judgment in order to avoid **stereotyping** this single mother as immoral and/or economically incapable of raising a family.

Instead, one must come to the **realization** that a family's ability to function is *not* dependent upon a predetermined value of "what a family should represent." From this learning comes the **recognition** that family lifestyles may exist in many different forms. Once the reason and acknowledgment behind personal discomfort becomes clear, the action necessary to remedy it becomes easier.

Trying to keep an open mind will help one to accept the different ways of thinking about life and of living from day to day. Honest self-examination will lead to a recognition of attitudes which interfere in the formation of an anti-bias way of thinking. More often than not, our opinions have been shaped by only limited

---

CHART 1.2

STEPS TOWARD RESPONSIVENESS AND EMPOWERMENT

Examination of Attitudes leads to →	Understanding of Personal Values and Biases
Acknowledgment of Attitudes leads to →	Awareness
Awareness of Attitudes leads to →	Self-Identity
Knowledge of Self leads to →	Appreciation of Self (Self-Esteem)
Appreciation of Self leads to a readiness of →	Respect for Others
Respect for Others leads to the creation of →	Responsiveness
Responsiveness leads to →	Empowerment
Empowerment to Address Bias leads to →	Affirmative Action
Affirmative Action leads to the ability to →	Change

Source: Valerie Rhomberg.

---

exposure to someone or something. Lack of knowledge and resources cause fear and create further negative attitudes. Accurate knowledge and **familiarity** with any of the areas of bias lessens the fear that usually accompanies ignorance.

Despite attempts to examine, address, and resolve discomforts, one may still have difficulty shedding them completely. Discomfort may well be intensified, for example, if the single mother were a teenager or a lesbian. Acknowledgment of uncomfortable feelings (in this case biases based on gender, belief, culture, class, and sexuality) becomes crucial. Acknowledgment leads to the awareness of a negative attitude and to the realization of the barrier it is causing.

PERSONAL BELIEFS

Does adhering to the anti-bias philosophy mean that personal beliefs are to be disallowed? It is important to acknowledge that everyone has many personal opinions. Not allowing personal feelings to be aired would be a bias in itself. (Censorship is, after all, an extension of bias.) However, a person who is placed in an influential position (such as a teacher) must always be aware that expecting others to have similar opinions, or trying to impose one way of thinking on others, will defeat the inclusionary concept of anti-bias education. The following concepts serve as a guideline for curriculum planning and modes of interaction:

- Differences are good.
- Differences do exist and can be enriching.
- One way is not necessarily the *only* way or the right way.
- The same thing can be done in many different ways.

Again, using the scenario of the single mother, interactions with a child from a family system of which one personally disapproves should not be any different from one's interactions with a child who comes from a family system of which one approves.

COMFORT LEVEL

The anti-bias approach promotes equal respect and acceptance within each area of bias. This does not mean that agreement with all the areas is required on the part of those involved. What is expected, however, is a level of familiarity and knowledge. Adults who work with children must acquire accurate information that enables them to deal with emerging issues of bias in such a way to ensure that children feel comfortable.

Achievement of a comfort level is what makes the pro-active component of this approach possible. It is this component, acquired through modelling of attitudes by adults, which empowers children to intervene sensitively and constructively when exposed to slurs, prejudice, or discrimination.

The anti-bias approach begins with adults. As adults free themselves from their own biased attitudes—a process that takes time, introspection, and patience—they achieve a comfort level with different values. Eventually this feeling of familiarity shifts into the pro-active dimension. This creates the possibility of a gradually emerging bias-free society, a society in which everyone feels good about themselves.

Diversity within the child's environment.

Strategy: The Use of Empowerment

Empowerment is a key component in the anti-bias approach. It is a tool through which society's inequities and biased attitudes are addressed and change can be effected. Both children and adults need to acquire the ability to be pro-active, respond in a constructive, nonviolent manner to any kind of injustice, be it implicit or explicit. This responsiveness shows itself through actions and/or words.

An anecdote shared with the authors illustrates that empowerment can be demonstrated as early as six years of age. Three six-year-old boys were playing together at one boy's house when they found a doll in a trunk. The two visitors immediately began making fun of their host, exclaiming, "Oooh, *you* play with dolls. Sissy!" The host boy responded: "You have a problem with that?" whereupon the other boys slowly disclosed that they, too, had played with dolls. Obviously, there was an adult in the host child's life who had conveyed to him a positive attitude toward nonstereotypical toys. His ability to stand up against stereotyping sprang from his strong sense of self.

In order for the anti-bias approach to work effectively, adults must:

- *Examine* honestly their own attitudes toward the 10 identified areas of bias.
- *Demonstrate* attitudes that acknowledge and affirm each child and adult in a positive manner.
- *Expose* children from infancy onward to an atmosphere that nurtures an awareness of and positive familiarity with diversity.

Within such an atmosphere of respect and acceptance, children will acquire feelings of usefulness and worth and become empowered to change situations for the better. Given the centrality of affective development, the anti-bias approach seems a relevant and logical choice when one is constructing the design of an early childhood education program.

WORKING IT THROUGH

❶ Diversity Bingo Game

This game (shown in Chart 1.3) can be used as an icebreaker to encourage participation and information sharing with one another. It is hoped that an atmosphere of comfort will ensue.

Purpose:

- to help participants recognize and label specific areas in which bias is found

- to assist participants in identifying anti-bias goals

Distribute a copy of the game to each participant. Instruct participants to find persons in the group who match one of the statements on the card. Boxes should be marked with an X when participants can match the description in the box with a Yes answer from someone in the group. Participants must find a different person for each statement. The first person with four

ANTI-BIAS AWARENESS BINGO CARD			
I feel very comfortable around people who look different. 1	I socialize with people whose sexual orientation differs from mine. 5	This is my first opportunity for self-examination regarding anti-bias. 9	My permanent residence has been something other than a house. 13
I help children recognize differences and similarities. 2	I participate in holiday celebrations with friends. 6	I know a house-husband. 10	I was an adult the first time I saw a person of another race. 14
I speak English and French. 3	I enjoy working with people of different ages. 7	I know a staff member who tells sexist jokes. 11	I display pictures of diverse abilities in my classroom. 15
I have a strong self-identity. 4	I have travelled to another continent. 8	I read legends from First Nations and Inuit cultures. 12	I help children challenge unfair situations. 16

CHART 1.3

Source: Adapted from *Roots and Wings* (1992), by Stacey York.

Xs in a row—vertically, horizontally, or diagonally—shouts out "Bingo." Reconvene as a large group and identify the areas/goals of anti-bias as represented by the statement in each square.

2 Small-Group Work—Article Analysis

Purpose:

- to help participants recognize and label specific areas of bias
- to help participants understand how biases are triggered
- to assist participants to devise solutions that could promote understanding and sensitivity to the issues of diversity
- to help participants realize why biases arise

Distribute the following excerpt (Box 1.1) and article (Box 1.2) to small groups of five. Ask each group to come to a consensus on the following questions.

1. What are the issues?
2. Which of the following 10 areas does each issue address (race, culture/ethnicity, gender,

sexual orientation, belief, age, ability, appearance, class, family composition)?

3. What attitudes are expressed in response to the issues?

4. What factors might be responsible for each of the attitudes identified?

5. What feelings do you think these attitudes would promote?

6. How could you work toward better understanding in the future?

Reconvene as a large group and share responses to the questions.

Collecting articles of a similar nature to have on hand for further discussions allows this exercise to be repeated focusing on current and topical issues.

Key points to address:

- overgeneralizations, stereotypes
- prejudice

- discrimination
- loss of something that is valued

Be prepared for the following participant responses:

- anger
- no response
- resistance
- agreement

Help participants explore reasons that may be contributing to these feelings. As participants become aware of their own values, assist them in seeing how these values influence their reactions and subsequent behaviours toward others.

Recommended source for further group work:

"Slurs, Stereotypes and Prejudice"
Hamilton Anti-Racism Committee
35 Catharine Street South
Hamilton, Ontario
L8N 4E8

BOX 1.1

"The proper family is a dutiful father, a stay-at-home mother and children," declares one woman firmly. "You can't build a country out of broken families."

Another woman says of mothers with paying jobs, "if they want a career, they shouldn't have children." A man adds: "The Bible outlines correct family values and it is our duty to live that way. Homosexuality is an abomination!"

Source: "Words to Live By," *The Toronto Star* (11 January 1994).

TROUBLES OF A NEIGHBOURHOOD IN FLUX

Won't learn English ... living 10 and 15 to a room ... mattresses from wall to wall ... oh! the smell ... urinating in the hall ... spitting, spitting, always spitting ... no respect for our laws ... the children swear at us ... the man said he was going to kill me ... damn politicians turned the neighbourhood into a refugee camp ... back where they came from ... cops here at three o'clock in the morning ... not a racist ...

They are engorged with rage and seething with resentment. The weight of their fury hangs heavy in the air, the babble of their complaints cresting, an eruption of outrage.

This is their gathering, here in the basement party room of a Dixon Rd. condominium complex, and their chance to testify.

"Where's the meeting being held?" one elderly woman had asked earlier, breathless after walking briskly across the courtyard. And another woman had put her finger to her lips, with a warning nod of her head toward the Somali family lounging on a bench. "Ssshhh."

It had begun almost furtively, with residents venturing down the stairs in ones and twos. But now there is no more room in the basement, the folding chairs are all occupied, and latecomers are leaning against the wall.

They are emboldened by their numbers and their shared grievances. They mutter each to each. They *understand* each other, because they live here, have for years owned condos here, have watched in disgust as this placid suburban community has been mutilated by a misguided immigration policy and hostile, filthy immigrants who sit around all day and *laugh* at the discomfort of the Canadians who were there first.

"We have lost our peace; we have no quiet enjoyment of our homes any more," a woman at the microphone is explaining in a pronounced Dutch accent. "I'm a taxpayer and I've lived here for 22 years. What I see now is anarchy and criminal behaviour. Can we not get across to these people the principle of freedom with responsibility?"

These people are the 3,000 Somalis who now occupy 35 per cent of the units in the York Condominium Corp.'s six buildings. Most other residents own their condos but the Somalis rent from absentee landlords. Many are refugees, "dumped here by the federal government," according to frustrated condo owners who have seen their property values plummet and their cozy existence ravaged by the newcomers' unfathomable behaviour.

They tell stories of excrement in the halls and children running through the corridors at all hours; of violent arguments and damaged property; of Somali women who glower at them when they try to explain the rules and Somali men who threaten them and Somali youths who frighten them. All these stories and more they recite to the bureaucrats and the officials, members of the Etobicoke mayor's task force, which

(continued)

BOX 1.2

was set up to find a solution after a violent melee last Friday between the Somalis and the condo corporation's security staff.

The main issue is overcrowding, everyone agrees: too many Somalis—extended families—shoehorned into small units. This may be natural for a tribal culture, the residents complain, but foreign and unacceptable to them. They are not, they insist, racist. They are concerned for their own investments and their own safety. This is *their* home and, dammit, they were here first. Says one woman, a real estate agent: "It seems like the words Dixon Road have been etched out there in the desert and everybody comes here."

It is interesting that almost everyone in this room—many of them older, retired—hails from someplace else. They are of all races and creeds and they claim to appreciate the immigrant experience. They wonder aloud why the Somalis won't assimilate a little more, won't *give* at all, won't even smile at them.

There's the black lady from South Africa, who moved to Canada 25 years ago. "If I could learn to abide by the rules of this country, so should the Somalis." And the gentleman from India who says the Somalis are "bred to mob violence." And the young Pakistani mother who grew up in this complex and returned to it after her marriage. "I am a Muslim myself. I wear traditional clothes in my home. But I feel like I'm being pushed into a corner, too. Why are *they* so aggressive toward *us?*" And this, from a middle-aged resident who sounded more bewildered than angry: "It's as if we don't exist for them."

In its specifics and its peculiarities, perhaps this simmering antagonism isn't about racial intolerance. At the very least, it is not that simple. There are wounded feelings on all sides; a tremendous distrust; suspicion. But just as a visitor begins to shed some of her preconceived notions about this dispute, another woman steps to the mike to speak her piece.

She is maybe 60 years old, prim, with silver finger waves and sensible shoes. Speaking in a heavy German accent, her voice drips with venom. "If the Somalis don't like our rules," she hisses, "they should go back where they came from. WE DON'T NEED THEM."

Everybody cheers.

– Rosie DiManno

Source: *The Toronto Star* (7 August 1993).

Appendix

MULTICULTURAL EDUCATION AND ANTI-BIAS, ANTI-RACIST EDUCATION

There has been much discussion about the differences between multicultural education and anti-racist education. While there are common, overlapping areas, differences do exist between the two approaches. These differences seem to be centred in the area of curriculum content and the locus of emphasis (Kehoe and Mansfield, 1993).

Curriculum content and the values that are transmitted to students (in any educational system) will usually reflect the dominant group, class, and gender within the system. Multicultural education uses the approach of exposing learners to the culturally diverse ways that people live in order to eliminate the predominant ethnocentric perspective and to make students aware that differences need to be accepted as valid (Aboud, 1988). Multicultural education works toward the goal of "intergroup harmony" (Kehoe and Mansfield, 1993, 4) by strengthening the individual's self-identity and by instilling pride in one's own ethnic heritage and respect for that of others. Prejudice and discrimination are fought on an individual basis.

Anti-racist education has as its focus "intergroup equity" (Kehoe and Mansfield, 1993, 4) and leads the learner through a curriculum which "includes the experiences and perspectives of Native and non-Western societies and people, described in their own voices" (Toronto Board of Education, 1991, 35). The emphasis in anti-racist education is twofold: (1) to make learners aware of systemic **racism** and its various manifestations within sociopolitical institutions, and (2) to challenge learners to confront and remove policies, practices, and materials that contribute to prevailing racist attitudes.

Anti-bias education falls somewhere in the middle of this educational continuum. The approach upholds a more *inclusive* definition of diversity than the other two, with the incorporation of, but not limited to, gender, ability, sexual orientation, age, and class in the curriculum. It supports the strengths of multicultural education by arguing that sensitive exploration of differences will create children whose self-identities are not threatened, and who will therefore be more respectful of others. It promotes the pro-active element of anti-racist education by encouraging children to take a stand against *any* discriminatory behaviour. In this way anti-bias education seems to fill the need for both intergroup harmony and equity.

CHAPTER 2

Exploring One's Values and Attitudes

PURPOSE

- *To explore how personal attitudes, values, and beliefs evolve through the examination of anti-bias issues*
- *To work through self-discovery and group processes involving choosing, prizing, and acting on values*

STRATEGIES

- *Exploration of attitudes and values via self-awareness questions, small- and large-group exercises, and independent projects*

MAKING THE CONNECTION

- *To identify how your values and attitudes may be prejudicial or biased, and how they create barriers in the implementation of anti-bias education*
- *To learn about yourself while actively listening to others describe their values and belief systems*

Exploring Values

A systematic examination of one's personal values and behaviour patterns is usually not undertaken for most adults entering the early childhood education profession. Yet the profession asks its practitioners to be attuned to and aware of how children acquire and construct knowledge and attitudes about self-identity and that of others. Limited self-knowledge hampers the interaction between teacher and child and impedes the process of anti-bias education.

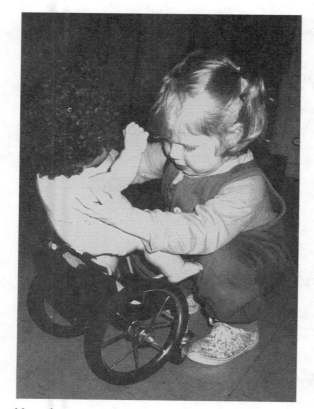

Natural curiosity and exploration of differences.

It is important to understand that as individuals we must first come to terms with our own identities before attempting to understand others. As Louise Derman-Sparks points out so eloquently, "What issues teachers see and hear from children, parents, and society, and what they choose to act on or ignore, are strongly influenced by their own cultural beliefs, unexamined attitudes, discomforts, and prejudice, as well as by their knowledge of children's development and learning and of societal biases" (Derman-Sparks, 1992). (See Diagram 2.1.)

In other words, the behaviours we demonstrate are a reflection of our values. Louis Raths developed a theory of values clarification that assists teachers and students not only to understand the process of valuing but also to sustain awareness of why we make the choices and take the actions that we do.

Raths identifies three primary processes that help shape an individual's value system:

- *Choosing*—selecting one's beliefs either freely or from a set of alternatives, with full consideration given to the potential consequences
- *Prizing*—recognizing, affirming, and living by a value we hold in high regard
- *Acting*—behaving in a manner that is consistent with one's beliefs so that a clear pattern emerges in one's life (Raths et al., 1978, 28)

For Raths, the term "value" can be upheld only if an individual has consciously met the criteria of all three processes. Raths outlines seven goals for individuals working with children. These suggestions have equal value for teachers in training, practising teachers, or any adults who would like to begin a more in-depth analysis of their value systems.

- Encourage children to make more choices, and to make them freely.
- Help children discover alternatives when faced with choices.

- Help children weigh alternatives thoughtfully, reflecting on the consequences of each.
- Encourage children to consider what it is they prize and cherish.
- Give children opportunities to affirm their choices.
- Encourage children to act, behave, and live in accordance with their choices.
- Help children become aware of repeated behaviours or patterns in their life (Raths et al., 1978, 38).

The following are possible areas to explore with children and adults:

Clothing: What statements are you making with the way you dress? What do you want others to think of you?

Leisure activities: What are your preferences and dislikes, and why?

Friends: What is important to you in choosing a friend? How do you sustain a friendship? What are your expectations of friendship?

Language: How do you use your speech? How could your choice of select words/phrases affect others? How often do you use words from another language? For what purpose?

Family: What are the important aspects of family? What are your expectations of family?

Money: On what basis do you prioritize your spending?

Vacation: What do you like to do? Where do you prefer to go? How do you like to get there?

Religion: In what way is it important to you?

Politics: Why do you affiliate with a particular political party?

The remainder of the chapter presents a compilation of exercises designed to assist individuals in discovering the process of valuing. (Many are exercises used in life skills/interpersonal relations courses and have no known authorship.)

The following exercises are divided into three major areas:

1. Self-awareness questions

2. Small- and large-group work (Choosing and Prizing)

3. Independent projects (Acting)

EXERCISE 1 Self-Awareness Questions

Focus: The suggested ways of presenting the self-awareness exercises include workshop format for professional development among supervisors and staff group, or as a basis for discussion between parents and educators. Alternatively, they may be integrated into the course content of teacher-training programs.

They will enable participants to explore their feelings and to describe their attitudes toward issues of bias. As well, they will increase participants' awareness of their attitudes and behaviours in addressing diversity and in countering bias. Each question can be adapted to ensure that the following areas are examined: race, ethnicity, socioeconomic status, gender roles, religious beliefs, sexual orientation, ability, age, appearance, and family composition.

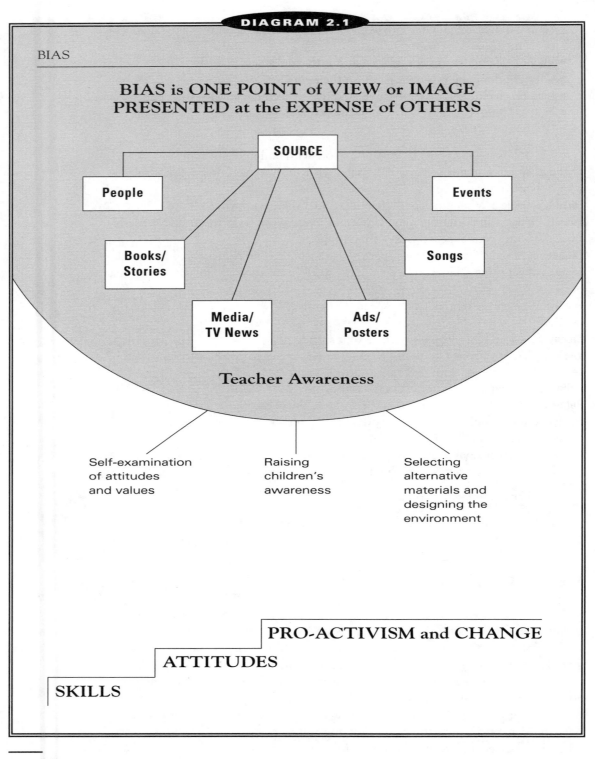

DIAGRAM 2.1

BIAS

BIAS is ONE POINT of VIEW or IMAGE PRESENTED at the EXPENSE of OTHERS

SOURCE

People

Books/ Stories

Media/ TV News

Ads/ Posters

Songs

Events

Teacher Awareness

Self-examination of attitudes and values

Raising children's awareness

Selecting alternative materials and designing the environment

PRO-ACTIVISM and CHANGE

ATTITUDES

SKILLS

Source: Adapted from McFarlane (1986).

1. Personal Examination and Awareness (Choosing and Prizing)

Method: Each participant engages in reflection by jotting down answers to the following questions and sharing their answers with the group. (This activity was developed by Louise Derman-Sparks.)

Questions:

1. What makes you who you are? Describe your racial, ethnic, and gender identity, physical ability, and appearance.
2. What aspects of your identity do you consider important for others to know about, and what aspects do you choose not to share? Why?
3. What specific incidents from your childhood may have shaped how you view yourself/your identity? What feelings are associated with these incidents?
4. What or who was influential in shaping your present attitudes toward your own background and toward people from different backgrounds?
5. If your feelings regarding your perceived identity have changed since childhood, who or what has contributed to this change?

2. Becoming Aware of How Stereotypes and Assumptions Are Created (Prizing)

Method: Each participant makes a list and shares those items with which they feel comfortable in the larger group setting. (This activity was developed by Ricky Sherover-Marcuse.)

1. What I want other people to know about my racial/ethnic/gender/class/religious identity.
2. What I don't want others to say about my racial/ethnic/gender/class/religious identity.
3. How I would prefer a person to acquire information about my culture; ways in which I appreciate how people are exposed to and learn about my culture.

Follow-up activity: Make two columns on the flipchart with headings titled:

1. Appropriate ways to learn about others
2. Inappropriate ways to learn about others

Participants are to share and record their ideas. Discuss methods that enable participants to learn about one another in an individualized, nonjudgmental manner, and contrast methods that are offensive and disrespectful.

3. Responses to Prejudice and Discrimination (Prizing and Acting)

Method: Participants write down one incident in which they have directly experienced discrimination or prejudice and how they responded. Next, participants write down an incident in which they witnessed prejudice and discrimination directed at someone else and how they responded. (This activity was developed by Louise Derman-Sparks.)

Question: What strategies did you use, and were they effective? If you didn't take action, what prevented you from doing so?

Follow-up activity: Large-group brainstorming taking up the shared information. Make two columns on the flipchart, one headed, "Obstacles to Acting" and the other "Effective Actions." Ask the group to identify obstacles and help them to reflect on the reasons behind their behaviour, e.g., fear of reprisal for interfering, which could take the form of job loss, physical harm, personal rejection, or threat to family safety. Explore the second column, asking participants to identify effective action strategies, enabling them to select those options they would feel comfortable implementing.

Remember that the larger goal of this exercise is to enable participants to recognize systematic bias (regardless of area) and to feel more confident in taking some form of action. Participants need to be aware of the process in which their own consciousness-raising has developed in order to facilitate this work of anti-bias education with young children.

Fitting in and feeling connected.

4. How Do I Fit in? (Prizing)

Method: Break the group into pairs, who interview one another using the following statements which reflect prizing. The topics that should be addressed are in parentheses next to each statement.

1. I am _____ and I value _____ (gender or racial background).

2. In my family, _____ is highly valued (family).

3. I expect _____ from my _____ (peers).

4. I celebrate _____ because _____ (culture).

In the debriefing period, sharing should be done from the pairs' perspective of "what I learned about ..." The facilitator should provide insight into how the group's memberships share many similarities and differences and the values attached to these.

EXERCISE 2 Small- and Large-Group Exercises

The small- and large-group exercises represent a broad cross-section of issues and dilemmas. Most of these activities will challenge individuals to reflect and affirm their beliefs and attitudes and force the participants to make choices and decisions in specific directions.

1. Value Analysis (Choosing)

Focus: This exercise will enable participants to gain awareness that various issues elicit different value responses. Participants will begin to build an acceptance of different viewpoints and gain understanding of the source of these values, attitudes, and beliefs.

Method: In groups of four, each member pulls out of a basket a value question relating to any of the areas of bias. Each member shares an opinion and a reason for this belief in response to the question. Emphasize that opinions need to be expressed in an atmosphere which fosters respect and open dialogue. At the end of the exercise, reconvene the large group for a broader discussion.

Sample value questions:

1. Do you think homosexuals should be permitted to work with young children, such as in child care, hospitals, schools, and family shelters? Why or why not?

2. How would you feel if your child/sibling decided to marry outside of your race? religion? class?

3. How would you feel if a parent who is physically challenged wished to do volunteer work at her child's child-care centre? Explain.

4. What neighbourhood in your city would you least like to live in? Why?

5. What would your first inclination be when seeing burn marks on the back of a toddler whose parents are considered prominent members of the community?

6. If you had to choose, who would you prefer to be?
   a) a person who is blind
   b) a person who is deaf
   c) a person who is paraplegic

7. If your son brought home his fiancée, what kind of woman would you approve of?
    a) one from a different race
    b) one who is 20 years older than your son
    c) one who is disfigured
    d) one who is from a poor family

8. How do you feel about women leaving their children in the care of others while pursuing a career? Why?

9. How do you feel about drug/substance-abusing mothers raising children? Why?

10. The local senior-citizens home would like to set up regular intergenerational visits to your child's preschool program. How would you feel about the arrangement?

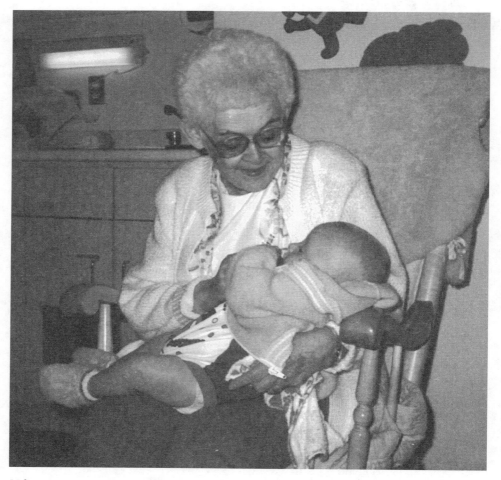

Valuing intergenerational nurturance.

Questions for a broader discussion:

What was difficult to hear without passing judgment?
Were you aware of why you had those reactions?
Can you identify their source?

──────
Source: Adapted from Simon et al., 1972.

2. Broken Squares (Prizing)

Purpose: This exercise gives participants the opportunity to engage in group **problem-solving** and cooperation. These skills must be communicated non-verbally. At the conclusion, the facilitator needs to point out how the participants' behaviours hindered or helped in resolving the task, and how lack of understanding or lack of awareness of others' problems poses barriers to group cooperation.

Method: Using Diagram 2.2 as a guide, the facilitator cuts squares of paper into pieces and then numbers each piece. The facilitator places all of the pieces labelled "1" into an envelope labelled "1," all of the pieces labelled "2" into an envelope labelled "2," and so on. Then the facilitator distributes the envelopes—envelopes 1 to 5 to one group of players, envelopes 6 to 10 to another group.

Now each group has a set of five envelopes, each envelope containing pieces of paper for forming squares.

When the facilitator gives the signal to begin, your group has the task of forming five squares of equal size. Your group has not finished until each person has a perfect square the same size as all the other squares.

During the exercise you must follow these rules:

1. Do not speak, point, or signal to others.

2. Do not ask for a paper from another group member.

3. Do not take a paper from another group member.

4. Do not signal for a paper in any way.

5. You may give a paper (or papers) to someone else.

Members may not throw their pieces into the centre for others to take; they must give the pieces directly to one other person. A member may give away all the pieces of his/her puzzle, even if he/she has already formed a square. The facilitator observes what happens and ensures that each member follows these rules.

Key points for follow-up discussion:

• How did it feel not being permitted to talk?
• How did not talking affect this activity?
• How did you feel when no one offered you a piece that you clearly needed?
• When did the group begin to cooperate?

DIAGRAM 2.2

BROKEN SQUARES

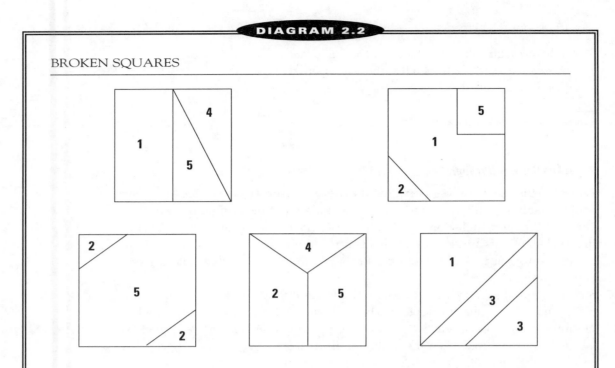

The facilitator inserts all of the pieces labelled "1" into the No. 1 envelope, the pieces labelled "2" into the No. 2 envelope, etc., and then distributes one set of five envelopes to each group of players.

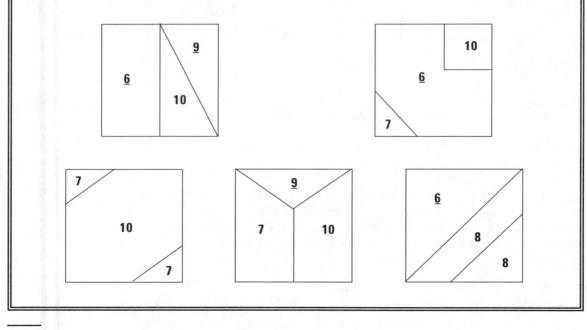

Source: Hall, Fontaine, Thompson, and Day (1993).

• How did you feel when others finished quickly? when you finished early?

Source: Louise Day, Native Child and Family Services, Toronto.

3. Cross-Cultural Role-play (Choosing)

Purpose: Participants will become aware of key areas in cross-cultural communication. Those role-playing as well as those observing will begin to assess the difficulties that arise in communication when members of each culture view others through their own values, attitudes, and behaviours. It is important that participants discuss not only differences in verbal and nonverbal behaviours but also their influence on the communication process.

Method: The task revolves around the need for a centre to welcome three new families. This is the first experience that staff have with families from another culture. The supervisor assigns staff members to be the contact teacher for each family. The staff are all Canadian-born. The facilitator divides the participants into three groups of three, with remaining participants as observers. Each group of three will be assigned individual roles: a teacher, a parent, and an observer. The person designated to role-play a family member will receive a communication sheet which they must enact accordingly.

N.B.: The communication sheets are a composite of a variety of cultural communication mannerisms and characteristics. No one culture is specifically reflected.

Roles: The teacher is conducting an orientation interview and welcoming the parent to the centre. The task for the teacher is one of gaining information and responding sensitively to the cultural mores.

The family member is responding to questions and obtaining information, while keeping in mind the designated cultural profile; please note the assignment of the following roles for females:

1. A female who has a submissive role and cannot speak directly to someone in authority. She defers to her husband, who must speak for her.

2. A female who is self-sufficient, independent, capable of negotiating and making decisions for herself.

3. A female who has to go back and check with her family prior to making a decision.

The observer will record objectively the verbal and nonverbal communication that is seen and heard between the teacher and the family member, and will note any areas of apparent discomfort.

The large group reconvenes when the interviews conclude, and the debriefing commences with the observer's findings. The teachers and the family members are allowed to contribute input which either corroborates or disputes the findings; both sets of players also have the opportunity to explain their feelings during this process.

The facilitator guides the discussion around areas which might reflect assumptions made on the part of the participants. The facilitator can create the communication sheets by selecting from any combination of the following characteristics:

Social distance

1. Three to four feet away

2. Very close

3. Female cannot sit next to a male

Eye contact

1. Impolite to look directly into speaker's eyes; eyes must be lowered or shifted because they are not allowed to focus on the speaker

2. Maintains strong eye contact as a sign of respect

3. Repeat of 1 or 2

Touch

1. Politeness is expressed by frequent patting or touching on the arm.

2. Handclasps or handshakes indicate honesty and pleasure.

3. Touching is not allowed because of religious beliefs.

Intervals in Speech

1. It is considered polite to begin speaking before speaker has finished to indicate attention to speaker.

2. Waiting 15 seconds before answer is given indicates thoughtfulness toward the speaker.

3. No initiation of answer unless spoken to directly.

Smile

1. No smiling in the presence of certain people (male or someone of a certain age) as it is considered disrespectful

2. Done for pleasure

3. Done in a forced manner to indicate agreement

4. What's Different About Me? (Prizing)

Purpose: Participants will begin to examine prejudging behaviours that may lead to discrimination and stereotyping. This exercise will enable participants to identify and acknowledge individual differences as a way to dispel stereotyping.

Method: Provide non-see-through plastic bags filled with bananas. The fruit should include different sizes, degrees of ripeness, colours, bruises, smells, stems, and any

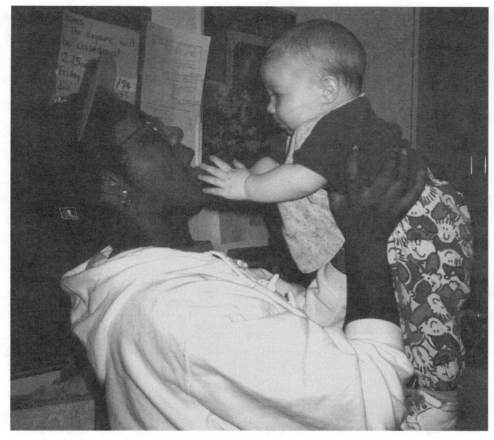

Getting to know one another.

other distinguishing marks. Have the bags of bananas passed from participant to participant and ask them to guess what is inside the bag. Ascertain how they know that they are bananas. What was the basis for their judgment (i.e., other's opinion, fact)? Afterward, have participants select their "own" banana, which they are not allowed to eat. Their goal is to get to know their personal banana with all its special features. After this careful examination, collect the bananas and put them in one pile. The participants must retrieve their own banana.

Questions: What made each person's banana unique?

How did participants feel about their banana's characteristics?

Did they believe they could find it again? How did it feel to do so successfully?

The facilitator should be ready to support any statements linked to prejudging and stereotyping people according to race or culture. If statements are not forthcoming, then the facilitator should raise this issue for discussion.

Source: Penny Corkum, The Hospital for Sick Children.

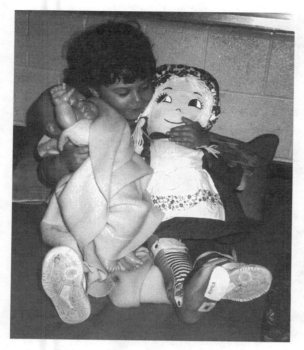

Differences don't really matter.

5. Bomb Shelter Problem (Choosing)

Purpose: This dramatic exercise forces participants to arrive at a decision that involves arguing for and making a choice based on what or who is considered valuable to our society.

Method: Participants should be divided into groups of 10 to problem-solve the scenario. Any participants who are left over can serve as objective observers and provide insightful commentary regarding behaviours during the group process.

The facilitator presents the following situation:

I have just been advised by the Department of External Affairs that a cruise missile travelling over the Arctic has gone awry and will soon drop on Saskatoon, Saskatchewan. The government has informed me that there exists only a limited number of bomb shelters across the country. Your group is lucky enough to be near a designated shelter. There is, however, only enough food, air, space, and water for six people to survive. The decision as to who goes and who remains behind is the task before you. As a group, you will have 20 minutes to arrive at a decision, keeping in mind the serious implications of this decision—these six people may be the only survivors in Canada.

You must come to a consensus. Try to make the most rationale choice in view of the fact that if you don't agree on the outcome, all 10 of you will perish. Here is a brief outline of your group's membership. Assign each participant one character from the cast.

MIYOKI – Japanese-born, Nobel Prize winner in chemistry, physically challenged, aged 32

CHRIS – White Anglo-Saxon, captain in the armed forces, specializes in nuclear-event survival techniques, homosexual, aged 40

OVID – Haida elder, aged 55

MARIE – French-Canadian, pregnant, high-school dropout, aged 17

COLIN – Political refugee from Somalia, oncologist on staff at a major hospital, aged 64

RACHEL – Rabbi, married to a professor in philosophy; she will not go without him, aged 37

JAMAL – Canadian, accountant, currently completing his CA certification, Jehovah's Witness, aged 26

TANYA – Polish-Canadian lawyer, atheist, aged 28

BORIS – Violinist and concertmaster with a world-renowned orchestra, Greek Orthodox, aged 41

DON – Canadian, National Hockey League player, aged 24

The facilitator gives warnings at the 15-, 10-, 5-, and 1-minute marks and concludes the exercise by slamming a door, indicating that the bomb has exploded. The groups share their results and reasons for the final selection, if made in time. The facilitator probes the group process with the expectation that a hierarchy of values will have been explored.

Any observers may comment on whether, within the group dynamics, there was bullying, stereotyping, pressuring, discrimination (and on what basis), how selections were made, the ability or inability to come to a consensus, and how these behaviours influenced the outcome. This exercise assists participants to clarify their own values.

Source: Adapted from Linda Silver, Canadian Mothercraft.

EXERCISE 3 Independent Projects—
Taking Action and Effecting a Change

Focus: The final stage of acting upon one's values and beliefs will be challenged through independent projects. Outcomes will depend in varying degrees on an individual's sense of self-esteem and the ability to find harmony between values and action.

Participants can initiate projects or select from a list of concrete experiences that will challenge existing personal or societal values. Participants will have to decide what level of action they feel comfortable implementing in order to act on issues that effect some kind of change.

Method: Provide a list of areas that require affirmative action or encourage participants to create their own list of three things they would like to change within their family, educational, or work setting. For those courageous few, there is also the government to tackle. Participants must identify the type of action they want to undertake and outline the steps necessary for implementation and evaluation of the outcome. The time frame is one month, with discretion given to more complicated actions, after which participants are expected to share their experiences.

Sample Projects

1. Interview residents, a social worker, and the coordinator of a shelter/hostel to understand some of the issues that people there face on a daily basis.

2. Visit several government subsidy offices around the city and observe the treatment of applicants.

3. Do a comparison of service delivery between an inner-city school and a public school in a well-to-do area.

4. Visit an ethnic area whose language is different from your own, and shop for breakfast and dinner items.

5. Use a wheelchair for a day and try to go about your daily business including using public transportation, grocery shopping, banking, picking up a child from school, etc.

Participants must be mindful of the treatment of people in relation to their age, gender, race, culture, class, ability, or appearance.

Source: Adapted from Simon et al., 1972, 257.

Potential Outcomes

Facilitators need to be aware of the possible responses these exercises will elicit. Participants may show a mixture of denial, anger, and resistance in varying intensities. Several factors should be considered in evaluating such responses:

- Past experiences are crucial. If as a child one was exposed to and had many opportunities to interact with diversity, then the emotional responses to this exercise are usually less intense and easier to deal with.
- Some people feel more strongly about certain areas than others. Sexual orientation is much harder to accept for many who might have been raised in a homogeneous community with traditional values.
- Adults who have travelled and lived in other countries tend to have a greater appreciation of differences than those who haven't experienced life in another culture.
- Assumptions that the facilitator from a dominant culture or power group can understand or empathize with experiences of participants from minority groups usually lead to greater resistance. This holds particularly true for more cosmopolitan centres such as Toronto, New York, and London.

Possible Strategies

The facilitator must establish an atmosphere of trust for open and honest dialogue to occur. She must allow different perspectives to be aired and disagreements to be discussed with the proviso that no one gets hurt. The struggle that ensues for the participants is the slow unravelling of how values and attitudes were formed. The next stage is learning how to deal with attitudes that are intolerant.

The following is an example from a discussion around stereotypes that emerged in response to the children's picture book *I'll Be You and You Be Me*. The main character is a child from an interracial family who is exploring what it would be like to be white. The child's hair is illustrated as spiky cornbraids standing up in all directions on her head. A black student remarked that this was a stereotypical portrayal of a black child. A white student responded by saying that many of her children wear "decorations" in their hair. The black student answered with a smile, "We are not Christmas trees. The child has barrettes in her hair."

This exchange reflects how different perceptions are formed dependent on past experiences. It also demonstrates the need for students to hear how others are perceiving and feeling images or statements. The realization that not everyone sees things from the same perspective is critical to developing the kind of sensitivity and respectfulness required when dealing with children and their families.

Summary

Perceiving, thinking, feeling, and behaving comprise the process of valuing. When a teacher works with children, her observations, decisions, interactions, and behaviours all emerge from her personal value system; this value system, in turn, influences children to choose, prize, and act in accordance with the teacher's values.

The preceding exercises assist any adult working with children to acquire four core skills necessary for teaching in an anti-bias fashion:

1. Listening and hearing with an open mind what children have to say.

2. Knowing how to place a child's comment in the context of developmental appropriateness. For example, a two-year-old who may react to the colour brown may seem to be prejudging but certainly is not demonstrating prejudicial thinking. The reason for his response could be causally related to his mother's attitude toward mud or warning about dog feces. A five-year-old, on the other hand, who makes the same comment may be showing prejudice. Teachers need to be aware when children are commenting on general colour versus social colour.

3. Knowing how to rephrase a child's comment nonjudgmentally. This skill requires the adult to echo a child's generalized statement by giving it a different slant and refocusing it on a specific issue. Here's an example:
Child: "I'm having a birthday party and I'm only having boys because we are going to do lots of sports."
Adult: "You're not inviting girls because you think they are not able to play sports as well as boys."

4. Being able to distance oneself emotionally when one's values are challenged by a hurtful comment or deed directed by children.

Example: You see a child pour a bucket of sand on top of a kitten's head. As an animal lover who prizes kindness to animals and who acts upon that value by volunteering on Sundays at the local animal shelter, your restraint is severely tested. The adult who can step back emotionally can enable the child to make the connection between his actions and the effect on the animal without compromising best ECE practice.

In summary, a person who has a positive self-identity can accept and respect differences in others without feeling threatened. A person who has a clear understanding of her own value system will be more open to value systems that might be different from her own. The person who has the ability to show mutual respect, to listen actively to others, to demonstrate an openness to new experiences and empathy for others, and finally to challenge the order of things for change will be guiding children's development in the anti-bias approach.

Learning to understand differences.

WORKING IT THROUGH

❶ Design a series of "values" questions for a preschool or school-age group (3–12 years). Try them out and record the children's answers. Summarize in developmental terms how the children are developing their self-identities and attitudes toward others.

❷ Personal Questions:

1. What aspect of your life is the most significant to you?

2. What actions might you take if this aspect were jeopardized?

3. How do you make others aware of the importance of this aspect?

CHAPTER 3

Living in a Diverse World with Sensitivity

PURPOSE

- *To discuss the skills needed by children and adults to work on the anti-bias approach of acceptance and respect*

STRATEGIES

- *To review developmentally appropriate skills for implementing anti-bias activity planning*
- *To define the skills adults need in order to support the development of children's ability to interact positively with diversity*

MAKING THE CONNECTION

- *To understand that anti-bias skills can be sequenced according to developmental abilities*
- *Anti-bias skills can be grouped into four major categories that assist in designing curriculum objectives:*
  - *1) Mutual respect*
  - *2) Active listening*
  - *3) Affective skill building*
  - *4) Pro-activism*

Multicultural Education Then and Now

Multicultural education as a pedagogical concept has seen a dramatic evolution over the past two decades. At its very core is the traditional premise of early childhood education—the nurturing of every child's self-identity and self-esteem so that children can grow and develop to their fullest potential.

The Canadian federal government's policy on multiculturalism (1971) and its Bill C-93 (1988) firmly rooted cultural and linguistic diversity as a strongly held value in Canadian society. In response, early childhood educators tackled the challenge of cross-cultural communication (Kehoe, 1984; Biocchi and Radcliffe, 1983), and offered strategies to overcome cultural biases (Chud and Fahlman, 1985). For the most part, however, multicultural education in Canada focused on the exotic aspects of food, festivals, and costumes.

The end of the 1980s saw the emergence of complex issues relating to social and economic change. Western society in the 1990s has witnessed large-scale shifts in ethnocultural demographics and family composition. Economic trends have given dramatic rise to social crises such as family violence, unemployment, crime, and racism.

These changes have prompted early childhood educators to challenge social inequities by heightening children's awareness of stereotyping and discrimination. The meshing of early-childhood and race-relations training has gradually emerged in a series of initiatives throughout Canada: Better Beginnings/Better Futures Project, 1990; Towards a New Response, Race Relations in Childcare Programs: Metro Toronto Forum, 1992; seminars and workshops on anti-racism in childcare, hosted by the Community Services Department of Nova Scotia and Child Care Connection (Virginia O'Connell); and teacher-training projects (Mock, 1988; Murphy Kilbride, 1990). The Early Childhood Multicultural Services in Vancouver, British Columbia, has given leadership since 1978 in the areas of pre- and in-service teacher training, public advocacy, research, and the development of multicultural and anti-racist resources. Changes in teacher-training curricula, both at the college and university level, have been exceedingly slow in comparison with the response from professionals in the field.

The diversity of values and issues of this decade have created a strong ripple effect on how educators carry out their responsibilities. The multicultural orientation used in the 1970s and 1980s has outgrown its earlier parameters. Educators are now required to have a more inclusionary approach to deal with the vast socioeconomic, political, and cultural differences that are evident in the young children and families with whom they work.

The focus of this chapter is to provide a bridge between theory (from the introductory chapter) and practice. This chapter will identify, from the child's perspective, the developmental goals required for each child's healthy emotional growth and the skills that each must master in order to interact positively with the areas of diversity. Similarly, the adult's perspective will be examined, in particular the requisite skills that support ongoing inclusion of diversity.

Diversity: How It Affects the Developing Child

Patricia Ramsey (1987, 193–94) initiated new perspectives on inclusiveness, outlining broad goals of teaching. They include the following:

1. The development of positive gender, racial, class, cultural, and individual identities.

2. The ability to identify, empathize, and relate with individuals from other groups.

3. Respect and appreciation for the ways in which other people live.

4. A concern and interest in others, a willingness to include others, and a desire to cooperate.

5. A realistic awareness of contemporary society, a sense of social responsibility, and an active concern for people outside of their immediate environment.

6. The autonomy to become critical analysts and activists in their social environment.

7. The development of educational skills and social knowledge that will enable them to become full participants in all aspects of society.

8. Effective and reciprocal relationships between homes and schools.

Ramsey's goals strongly link the issue of diversity with a child's affective development. Teacher preparation has been negligent, however, by omitting this vital connection when discussing child development. Similarly, new teachers are not taught to apply the attitude of inclusiveness in curriculum design. The thematic approach, which is the traditional method taught to students, is severely limiting when exploring areas of diversity. To be effective, curriculum design must support key developmental goals that will enable children to live in a diverse society.

The progression of cognitive and affective developmental abilities is a gradual and predictable one from infancy through to the school-age years. For example, children are unable to see themselves as separate and autonomous until they have mastered such cognitive and affective milestones as object permanence and individuation. These milestones are usually consolidated by the end of the toddler years. Understanding how one person can be a girl, Jewish, of Argentinian background, Canadian by nationality, or belonging to the middle class is beyond the mental ability of the preschooler who is still mired in egocentric thinking and unable to classify using more than one physical attribute. Educators need to be mindful, therefore, of the developmental constraints that make learning about anti-bias a slow and thoughtful process.

Goals of the Early Childhood Educator

According to Louise Derman-Sparks, four developmental goals frame the design of any curriculum that sets out to build the attitude of inclusiveness. The following section presents these four goals, each of which is followed by an analysis of specific developmental expectations that must be mastered before that goal can be attained (adapted from Derman-Sparks, 1992).

Goal 1: To foster each child's construction of a knowledgeable, confident self-identity.

This goal includes both personal and group identity, for many children a bicultural identity. It means fostering confidence, not superiority (Derman-Sparks, 1992, 118).

Fostering a knowledgeable, confident self-identity.

BOX 3.1

DEVELOPMENTAL EXPECTATIONS—CONFIDENT SELF-IDENTITY CAN BE REALIZED WITH THE FOLLOWING:

▶ recognition of individual physical characteristics

▶ recognition of gender; attainment of gender constancy

▶ recognition of self as separate and autonomous

▶ recognition of physical abilities

▶ recognition of self in relation to the family, i.e., language, customs, behaviours, racial identity

▶ attainment of racial constancy

▶ recognition of self in relation to the group, i.e., peer, ethnic, racial, and class

▶ recognition of self in relation to larger social networks, such as community, city, and country

Goal 2: To foster each child's comfortable, empathetic interaction with diversity among people.

This goal includes developing the disposition as well as the knowledge to understand and appreciate differences and similarities among people, to respectfully

BOX 3.2

DEVELOPMENTAL EXPECTATIONS—COMFORTABLE, EMPATHETIC INTERACTION WITH DIVERSITY CAN BE REACHED WITH THE FOLLOWING:

▶ recognition of similarities and differences in physical characteristics, abilities, social behaviours, and language

▶ the ability to classify using more than one attribute

▶ understanding of class inclusion

▶ the gradual decrease of egocentrism and increase in the ability to see another's viewpoint

Experiencing comfortable interaction with differences.

and effectively ask and learn about differences, and to comfortably negotiate and adapt to differences (Derman-Sparks, 119).

Goal 3: To foster each child's **critical thinking** about bias.

Thinking seriously about bias means developing the cognitive skills to identify unfair and untrue images (stereotypes), comments (teasing, name calling), and behaviours (discrimination) directed at one's own or another's identity—whether gender, race, ethnicity, disability, class, age, weight, or other characteristics—and the emotional empathy to know that bias hurts (Derman-Sparks, 120).

Goal 4: To foster each child's ability to stand up for herself/himself and for others in the face of bias.

Confronting bias means helping each child learn and practise a variety of ways to speak up when

a) another child acts in a biased manner toward her or him

b) a child acts in a biased manner toward another child

c) an adult acts in a biased manner

Goal 4 builds on Goal 3. Critical thinking and empathy are necessary components of acting for oneself or for others in the face of bias (Derman-Sparks, 121).

BOX 3.3

DEVELOPMENTAL EXPECTATIONS—CRITICAL THINKING ABOUT BIAS CAN BE ACHIEVED WITH THE FOLLOWING:

▶ the ability to see a whole and its parts separately

▶ the ability to decode, compare, and think critically about people, objects, and events in positive and negative terms

▶ the ability to begin problem-solving on an abstract level

▶ the ability to begin predicting outcomes based on direct experiences

DEVELOPMENTAL EXPECTATIONS—CONFRONTING BIAS CAN BE ATTAINED WITH THE FOLLOWING:

▶ the ability to express ideas and feelings in socially acceptable ways

▶ the ability to comprehend stories and interpret characters' actions, feelings, and ideas

▶ the ability to initiate, plan, and organize actions in accordance with a belief or value

As early childhood educators, we must ensure that children have the opportunities to practise the specific skills related to the developmental challenges addressed above. These skills should guide our decisions in curriculum design. Chart 3.1 illustrates such a range of skills found in the cognitive, affective, and language domains.

Planning for Anti-Bias Skills

As teachers evaluate curriculum experiences for their contextual and developmental *relevance*, they can also identify which anti-bias skills are being practised. Anti-bias skills are developmentally linked to the curriculum goals just discussed. These skills evolve in a developmental progression and can be grouped into four major categories: mutual respect, active observing and listening, skill building, and pro-activism. The four categories reflect primarily the affective domain, although cognitive objectives are required. Used as a guideline, they enable teachers to promote anti-bias attitudes and skill development.

Adapting and scrounging materials to implement these goals.

CHART 3.1

SUMMARY OF DEVELOPMENTAL SKILLS

COGNITIVE

observing
object permanence
object constancy
discrimination (notice
    similarities/differences)
generalizing
imitation
matching
cause and effect
classifying
comparing
problem-solving
constructing relationships
    between objects/
    people/events
centration
reversibility
memory
sequencing
gathering information
distinguishing between
    fantasy and reality
exploring rules
critical thinking/evaluation
differentiating specific ideas
categorizing
synthesizing
predicting outcomes
adapting
internalizing another's point
    of view
making judgments
organizing, initiating,
    planning
group activism

AFFECTIVE

separation and individuation
trust
egocentrism
helping
cooperation
turn-taking
sharing
empathy
respecting and valuing
    others
tolerance
ability to be inclusive
self-control
self-confidence
initiative
awareness of
    responsibilities

LANGUAGE

naming/labelling
identifying objects, people,
    feelings
listening comprehension
describing abstract qualities
    and ideas
asking questions
explaining
drawing conclusions
making inferences
acknowledgment of
    unfairness
expressing opinions
intervening
negotiating
challenging
conflict resolution

Source: Nadia Hall.

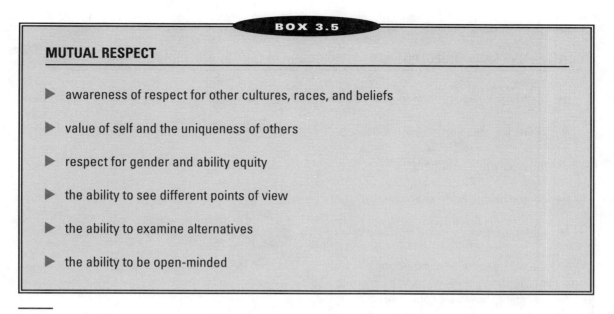

BOX 3.5

MUTUAL RESPECT

▶ awareness of respect for other cultures, races, and beliefs

▶ value of self and the uniqueness of others

▶ respect for gender and ability equity

▶ the ability to see different points of view

▶ the ability to examine alternatives

▶ the ability to be open-minded

Source: Adapted from York, 1992.

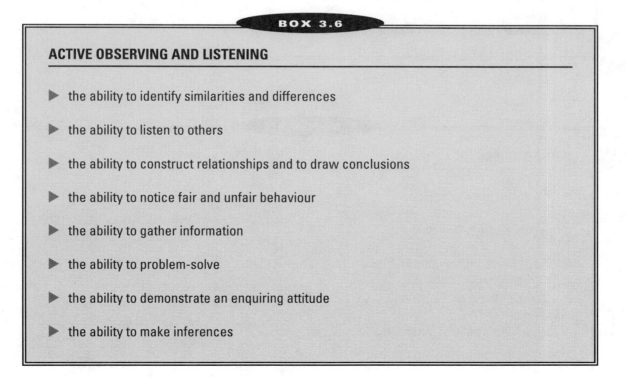

BOX 3.6

ACTIVE OBSERVING AND LISTENING

▶ the ability to identify similarities and differences

▶ the ability to listen to others

▶ the ability to construct relationships and to draw conclusions

▶ the ability to notice fair and unfair behaviour

▶ the ability to gather information

▶ the ability to problem-solve

▶ the ability to demonstrate an enquiring attitude

▶ the ability to make inferences

Source: Adapted from York, 1992.

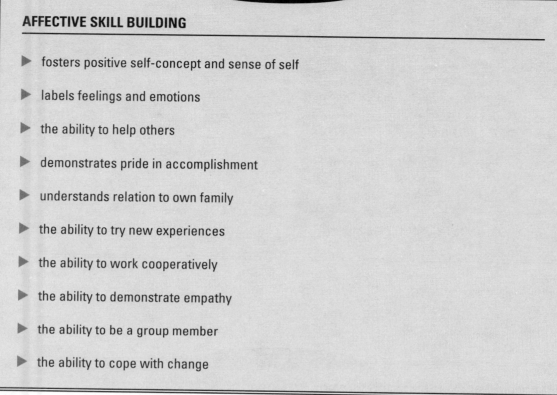

BOX 3.7

AFFECTIVE SKILL BUILDING

▶ fosters positive self-concept and sense of self

▶ labels feelings and emotions

▶ the ability to help others

▶ demonstrates pride in accomplishment

▶ understands relation to own family

▶ the ability to try new experiences

▶ the ability to work cooperatively

▶ the ability to demonstrate empathy

▶ the ability to be a group member

▶ the ability to cope with change

BOX 3.8

PRO-ACTIVISM

▶ the ability to make choices

▶ avoids name-calling, teasing

▶ the ability to challenge stereotypes

▶ participates in group action

▶ takes action against unfair situations or comments

Source: Adapted from York, 1992.

Affective skill building requires enriched perspectives on diversity.

Awareness and respect for other cultures.

Chapters 7–10 Illustrate in depth the application of these anti-bias skills in activities designed for infants, toddlers, preschoolers, and school-age children.

Skills for Adults

The scope of an adult's influence on how children view the world is determined by what a teacher does and does not do. Teachers can enhance children's perspectives on diversity or they can negatively impact on children's interactions with it. It is important, then, that each of the adults involved in children's daily lives acquires and continually improves those skills that will facilitate implementation of an anti-bias approach.

For children to function with respect in a world of diversity, they need adults who will offer them opportunities to:

- be provided with correct information
- be exposed to diversity
- be made familiar with areas of bias
- build a comfort level with differences
- be able to acquire empathy
- challenge stereotypes
- support activism when challenged

DIAGRAM 3.1

AFFECTIVE SKILL BUILDING

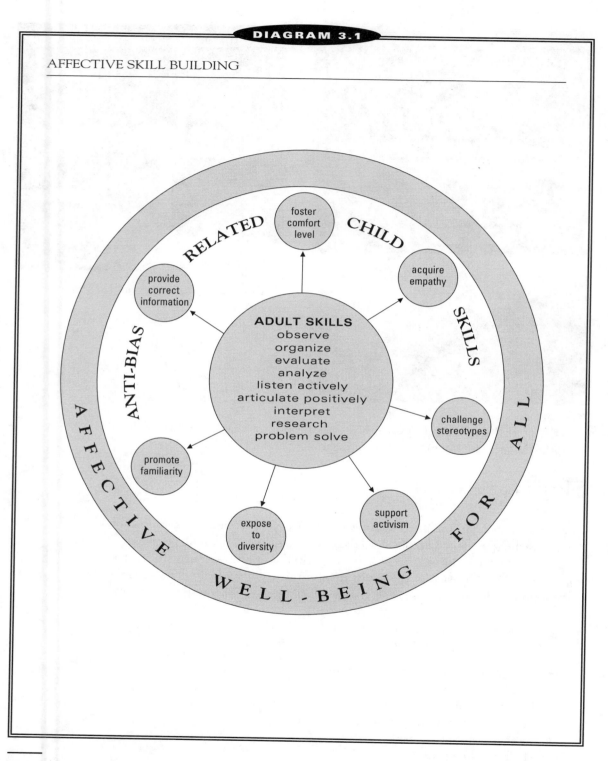

Source: Hall and Rhomberg.

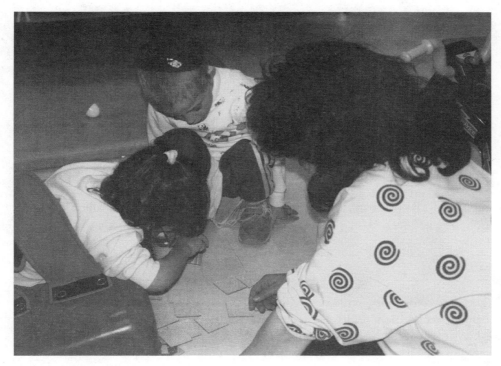

Playing together, learning together.

THE ROLE OF OBSERVATION: OBSERVE, ORGANIZE, ANALYZE

One of the fundamental skills required by teachers is the capacity to be acute observers. *Observation* skills make it possible for adults to assess the interaction between the physical and personal environment based on children's actions and words. Looking and listening carefully are closely linked to *organization* and *analysis*. Analysis of the physical environment leads to a clearer organization of its components as teachers strive toward fostering interactions with diversity in all program areas. Similarly, analysis yields a more sensitive selection of materials in order to expose children to different areas of bias, challenge stereotypes, promote personal interactions—among children, between adults and children, and among adults— that build inclusionary attitudes.

RAISING AWARENESS: LISTEN, INTERPRET, EVALUATE

The communication skills of *active listening* and positive explanation assist families, children, and other adults to hear interpretation of messages correctly from all those involved with the educational program. The ability to *interpret* messages nonjudgmentally goes hand-in-hand with the ability to challenge discrimination in a positive and nonthreatening manner. Both of these skills are vital in modelling pro-activism. Altogether these skills build not only the self-esteem but also a positive sense of well-being of all participants.

RESEARCH: RESEARCH, PROBLEM-SOLVE

The development of strong *research* skills and *problem-solving* abilities are necessary for adults as they endeavour to broaden children's knowledge with correct information about the many facets of human differences. In this way misconceptions and negative assumptions are replaced with a comfort level—one that is mandatory if children are to become empathetic toward all areas in which bias occurs, a comfort level that contributes to the children's ability to challenge unfairness and utilize action to bring about change.

The correlation is clear. For children to acquire the skills to live in a diverse, global society with sensitivity, it is necessary for adults to be vigilant in their observations, evaluations, interpretations, research, organization, and presentation of materials. The degree to which these skills are present profoundly affect the emotional well-being and, most importantly, the self-esteem of all those involved.

Summary

The task before early childhood educators is to nurture inclusionary attitudes and behaviours within the diverse population of their programs. The dilemma arises when teachers themselves are not in touch with their own feelings toward certain areas of bias. For teachers who work in larger cities such as Toronto, Montreal, or Vancouver, dealing with issues that stem from working with multiracial, multi-ethnic families or children of same-sex couples is a reality. How they will respond to these issues is an ongoing challenge. But for teachers who live in areas with more homogeneous populations, this reality becomes more hypothetical, thus dealing with it tends to be avoided.

No matter what type of environment the teacher finds herself in, she must never lose sight of the educational objective and developmental goals that place the anti-bias approach firmly within the design of the affective curriculum.

Recognition of self in relation to family.

WORKING IT THROUGH

1 Small-Group Work—Analysis and Intervention

Below are five scenarios that represent different areas of bias. For each scenario:

a) Identify the issue.

b) Identify the child(ren)'s developmental level and abilities within the anti-bias context (refer to pages 45–46).

c) State the area(s) that will be affected by this situation.

d) Identify what adult skills you would use in response to the children's behaviour/statements.

e) Evaluate all this information and devise an intervention strategy that promotes an anti-bias approach.

Scenarios

1. Just before recess, a teacher hears two seven-year-old boys talking.

   White child: "Hey, Bobby, if you wanna come with me to get candy, you better remember to keep your hands out of your pockets. Oh, yeah, and don't bring nothing into the store 'cause the guy will think you stole it."

   Black child: "Yeah, yeah, I know. My mom is always bugging me about that stuff."

2. Driving home in a car pool with three four-year-olds in the back seat, a parent overhears her child whisper to another child: "Don't talk to Rhonda, 'cause she talks funny." They then begin to giggle. The parent notices Rhonda's sad expression in the rear-view mirror.

3. In the dramatic play area two four-year-old boys and one five-year-old girl are playing with the props. Gary says to Chris, "We're going to get married. Right, Chris?" The girl replies, "My mommy says boys can't get married. Besides, you don't look the same. Gary has funny eyes and Chris is a brown colour." An argument among the three ensues.

4. A restaurant is set up in the dramatic play area. A three-year-old boy sits at the table and a young girl is cooking:

   Boy: "You bring me the tea. You're the girl."

   Girl: "No, I want to sit down. Adam, you make the tea."

   Boy: "Okay."

   Another boy: "No, Adam. You sit down. Girls do the cooking and Daddy's work."

5. A teacher who pays meticulous attention to her own appearance comments to a five-year-old child, in front of another child, "I see you haven't had time to brush your hair today. Why don't you try using a ponytail holder like Sheila."

N.B. Specific communication strategies and explanations for appropriate and inappropriate techniques are presented in Chapter 6.

❷ Individual or Small-Group Work—Designing a Checklist

Programming and environmental design require ongoing evaluation and modification. Design a checklist that would enable you to monitor how and to what degree you are reflecting the anti-bias approach in your physical and personal environment, e.g., (1) Do I have people-coloured crayons, paints, paper, felt, and play-dough out on a consistent basis? (2) Do I challenge the children to identify stereotypes or discriminatory behaviour in books?

Curriculum Design for an Anti-Bias Program

PURPOSE

- *To explore the practical application in designing an anti-bias curriculum that meets the developmental needs of children from infancy through school age*

STRATEGIES

- *Examination of thematic and developmental approaches to programming*
- *Webbing and exploring related ideas and experiences*
- *Integration of anti-bias skills in activity planning*

MAKING THE CONNECTION

- *Awareness of the importance of matching anti-bias skills with developmental level and contextual relevance*
- *Practitioners have a choice of program approaches. Anti-bias skills can be woven into either developmental or thematic programming*

Designing the Curriculum

Volumes have been written on the subject of curriculum development. There exists a variety of models based on different interpretations of learning theories and instructional approaches. The National Association for the Education of Young Children (NAEYC) position paper "Developmentally Appropriate Practice in Early Childhood Programs Serving Children from Birth through Age 8" (Bredekamp, 1987) gives clear guidelines for appropriate and inappropriate practices for such program elements as curriculum goals; teaching strategies; guidance of socioemotional, cognitive, and language development; skillful interactions; and environmental design. The essence of this approach is child-directed learning and informal teaching. In this perspective, the child interacts with objects and people in an environment which offers stimulating and challenging play materials. This approach also relies heavily on mediation by attuned developmental specialists, the theory that is commonly encouraged in most Canadian colleges.

Students are instructed to view curriculum as a triangular relationship with the three major vertices of *learner*, *content*, and *process* interconnected. The relevance and developmental appropriateness of a teacher's program will be ensured if the teacher considers and continually evaluates *who is being taught, what is being taught,* and *how it is being taught* (Feeny et al., 1991, 228).

In this chapter discussion is divided into two major areas of interest:

1. the two predominant approaches of curriculum planning
   a) theme-based planning
   b) developmental-based planning

2. webbing, exploring strands and experiences

Curriculum Planning

THEME-BASED CURRICULUM PLANNING

This is a highly organized approach which allows teachers to provide a focused and integrated exploration of an idea. The benefit of this approach is that children can engage in active play and challenging experiences across all developmental areas, thus making connections from different perspectives. A week of exploring "garbage" can include, for example :

- a dramatic play area that is converted into a kitchen with different blue boxes, a composter, and a variety of boxes and containers reflecting different cultural foods and scripts
- gross-motor activities that focus on outdoor walks to pick up litter; transporting garbage or compostables in wagons and tricycles; visiting a garbage dump
- classification is readily carried out as children group recycled garbage according to type: cans, plastic, paper/cardboard; similarly, what foods can and

cannot be composted lends itself to classification
- related songs, stories, and imaginary tales
- creative, sensory experiences can be done by turning the sand table into a composter; add earth along with orange and apple peels, eggshells, and coffee grinds; painting can be carried out with eggshells while box sculpture challenges problem-solving abilities

What has the child learned?

Altogether, these experiences gradually contribute to the child's knowledge of and understanding about his responsibility to the environment. The scope of knowledge and the level of developmental challenge presented are assessed by the teacher as part of the planning process.

DEVELOPMENTAL-BASED CURRICULUM PLANNING

This approach to curriculum design focuses exclusively and systematically on supporting developmental tasks and milestones. Teachers are well versed in the age-related sequence of skills that become the foundation of the curriculum. A benefit of this approach is its highly individualized orientation. Planning is driven by observations of children's emerging abilities and interests. Flexibility is key in its implementation. Sensitive attunement to the different needs across all the developmental domains ensures skillful attention to each child's ongoing development.

DEVELOPMENTAL DOMAINS: INFANCY TO PRESCHOOL

A brief outline of the developmental domains follows, in its progression from infancy to the preschool period. This will assist the reader to move to the secondary stage of planning.

Gross Motor This domain requires coordination of the body's large muscles, beginning with the ability to hold the head upright and progressing through to standing and moving independently through space. Balance, posture, smooth and coordinated movement, as well as muscular strength, need to be observed and supported. The final goal is for the child to integrate and execute whatever motor planning is required for an activity.

Fine Motor This domain involves the sequential development of all small-muscle movement including eyes, mouth, hands and arms, eyes and hands, progressing from reflexive, nongoal-directed actions to the mastery of purposeful reach, grasp, release, and finally to the manipulation of objects of all different shapes and sizes. Fine-motor planning requires thought given to the timing of a movement, location of the object in space, and an understanding of the functional relationship between body parts and the object.

Language The sequence of skills is acquired cumulatively in this domain with the awareness that auditory-receptive abilities are developed first. It is important to the development of communication that learning occurs strongly at the receptive level, i.e., hearing and selection of auditory cues from among background noise; storage and retrieval of certain sounds that have acquired specific meaning or purpose; and comprehension of auditory symbols or words. Once the speech organs and respiratory coordination are in place, expressive skills will begin to develop. The predictable sequence includes: vocalization, babbling, holophrastic sentences, telegraphic speech with proper intonation for questions or demands, and the final functional level whereby a child has the ability to coordinate words using appropriate syntax to express ideas and feelings.

Cognitive The development of this domain progresses from the general exploration and understanding of concrete objects perceived through all the senses (dependence on the presence of physical materials) to understanding symbolic ideas conveyed through pictures or words, either spoken or written. The child slowly moves away from perceptual dependence toward abstract mental images supplied by memory of experiences and factual information.

This area of human development is guided by the child's ability to organize his attention and behaviour in response to the environment. The ability to sort out relevant stimuli from distracting stimulation occurring in the environment is essential for focus and attention. The ability to sustain attention long enough to achieve a goal is critical to problem-solving and learning. Directing attention, persistent focus, and level of motivation in order to reach a goal are found in varying degrees in children. The degree to which they are used significantly affects how a child learns and the successful acquisition of developmental skills.

Socioemotional The development of a secure, confident child who has the ability to form warm, trusting, and intimate relationships with others has its beginnings in infancy. Positive sense of self builds on cumulative experience of having needs met consistently and promptly, while self-esteem grows in response to mastering new skills and handling challenges with increasing effectiveness. Key areas to support are: attachment needs to the family; bids for autonomy; the developing awareness of an identity that includes gender, race, and ethnicity; and social interactions that build feelings of empathy and respect among peers.

WEBBING

Once an approach has been selected, the next step in the planning process is called webbing. It is a widely used tool which assists the teacher to think divergently about a theme. A theme can be broken down into many concepts. A concept is then considered a strand in terms of the developmentally appropriate activities that can then be generated. Each strand reflects and interweaves an extended relational idea. Altogether, each thread of the web enriches and expands children's growing understanding of the world and their place in it.

For example, webbing the theme "water" could yield these various related concepts: weather, transportation, occupations, functional uses, animals, bodies of water, and scientific, physical processes. Activities that encourage children to explore these concepts are, again, designed and presented in harmony with the guidelines that frame developmentally appropriate learning.

Webbing from the developmental-based approach focuses instead on learning outcomes. Developmental tasks such as problem-solving, sequencing, patterning, relational thinking, symbolic play, perceptual motor skills, and expressive and receptive language abilities are central to a teacher's planning (Hall, 1993). Discussion of this topic as it relates to infant/toddler curriculum is explored in the next chapter.

Diagrams 4.1 and 4.2 represent examples of webbing using the two distinctive approaches discussed. The theme Patterns and Rhythms has been selected to demonstrate the evolution of an anti-bias curriculum plan.

Patterns and Rhythms

THEME-BASED WEBBING (See Diagram 4.1.)

The theme-based webbing process follows five steps:

1. Select a theme for exploration.

2. Web as many concepts and related ideas as possible.

3. Design activities that support exploration of these ideas.

4. Organize these activities into the primary content areas that direct the program. The core content areas are:

   - Math/Manipulatives
   - Environmental Studies (incorporates science, community, and values/attitudes)
   - Language (includes music, literature, dramatic activities)
   - Creative/Perceptual Motor
   - Gross Motor/Movement

Each activity will contribute another perspective on the theme Patterns and Rhythms.

5. Organize the activities into a weekly program plan. The plan should reflect an integrated and sequential approach to learning about the theme.

Five major concepts are identified in the webbing diagram that was devised for the theme Patterns and Rhythms. They are: the Senses, Family, Life Cycle, Natural Elements, and Temporal Relations. Each concept was broken down further into related ideas that still support the primary focus of patterns and rhythms.

1. The senses: visual and tactile patterns (colour, texture, form, and movement); auditory rhythms (pitch, tempo, and repetition); olfactory and gustatory (things look the same but have different smells and tastes).

2. Life cycle: animals, humans, plants all follow a similar rhythm in the life cycle; humans exemplify diversity in appearance, ability, and age; plants can be grown in different environments; they are varied in appearance, taste, smell, and function.

3. Family: the pattern of family life is reflected in the diversity of language, composition, clothing, food, music, friends, games, leisure or art activities, routines, etc.

4. Natural elements: the natural elements of air, water, earth, and objects in space all demonstrate patterns and rhythms.

5. Temporal relations: the rhythm of time is felt in the seasons and diurnal and nocturnal routines.

The next step is to generate activities which will enable children to practise such developmental skills as experimenting, testing, and comparing as they work individually or in small groups on these experiences.

Some sample activities under the Family concept include:

- exploration of different types of homes; provision of different types of beds for dolls
- different footwear and bags in the dramatic prop box
- sharing of different nocturnal routines in families
- different family relationships
- different ways of carrying babies
- different games people play as infants, preschoolers, school-age children, and adults
- listening to different stories and songs that are specific to families
- different ways of communicating (signing, talking in different languages)

The patterns and rhythms of "family" assist children to investigate and draw relationships between themselves, other people, and objects in their world.

Visual patterns can include colour and shapes in fabric mâché, paper folding, weaving, lacing, printing, puzzles, tangrams, pegboards, hair colour and styles, and skin colours. Form, especially symmetry, can be compared in nature.

Tactile patterns can be explored in feely boards, Braille letters, sand/playdough/water play with patterned utensils, hair textures, and natural objects.

Objects representing diversity in families.

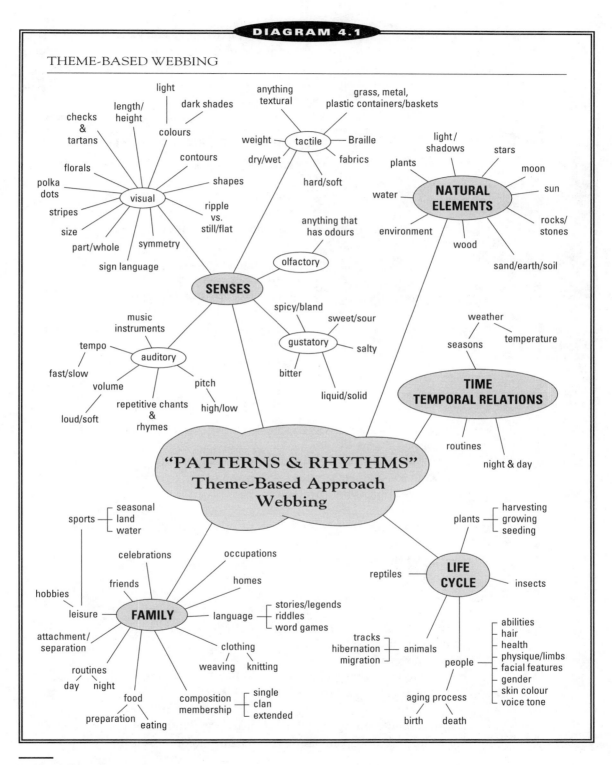

DIAGRAM 4.1

THEME-BASED WEBBING

"PATTERNS & RHYTHMS" Theme-Based Approach Webbing

Source: Hall and Rhomberg.

Auditory rhythms and patterns in pitch can be compared in various clapping games, culturally diverse songs, musical instruments, rhymes, nonsense poems, and stories with repetitive patterns.

The distribution of representative activities among the content areas will look like this:

Collect and make manipulatives to represent all the areas of bias.

THEME: PATTERNS AND RHYTHMS

MATH/MANIPULATIVES

puzzles
tangrams
dominoes
buttons of varied shape, colour, size, and
    number of holes
patterned popsicle sticks
blocks (different shapes and sizes)
unpopped, coloured popcorn
scale with gourds, stones, pine-cones, nuts, etc.
lotto "script" cards
texture boards

ENVIRONMENTAL STUDIES

cooking—various textures, spices to taste
washing and drying clothes
planting and the growth cycle (in water and in soil)
water and ice, and temperature influences
life cycle of animals/humans (aging process)
types of homes
types of transportation
friends of all ages
routines of the day

LANGUAGE

riddles
chants—in different languages
rhymes/nonsense poems
books with repetitive patterns such as *3 Billy Goats Gruff, Good Morning Owl,*
    Runaway Bunny, Mommy Buy Me a China Doll, etc.
songs and finger plays with repetition, and in different languages
learning hello/goodbye in various languages (including signing)
felt board stories adapted or original to relate to concepts being explored

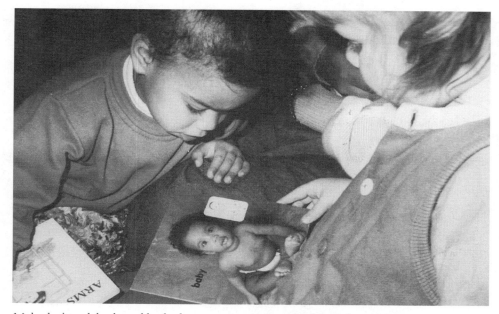

Make dual-track books and books demonstrating signing part of the daily reading routine.

CREATIVE/PERCEPTUAL MOTOR

painting: feather, sponges, sand, yarn, bark
weaving: fence, looms, dream catcher, God's eye
rubbings
beading
braiding
signing
folding clothing
water play with different holed utensils
Braille mats
construction of shelters/homes: Kwakwitl community house, jip, Hopi pueblo,
    Benin tree house, boathouse

GROSS MOTOR/MOVEMENT

follow pathways/tracks of different animals
toe puppets
dances of different cultures
walking on snowshoes, crutches, stilts
shadow tag
hopping/skipping games
follow-the-leader patterns

DEVELOPMENTAL-BASED WEBBING (See Diagram 4.2)

The alternate method of curriculum design is comprised of three steps:

1. Teachers link observations of the children and their developmental needs to determine the direction of the programming.

2. Teachers select objectives from the broad range of developmental skills found in Chapter 3.

3. Teachers select an appropriate content area which will support the practice of the developmental skill.

The process for designing activity experiences in the developmental-based approach is reversed. The teacher identifies the skills that children need to practise and then organizes experiences to capitalize on these opportunities. The list of sample activities is categorized according to developmental objectives, although they reflect the same focus of patterns and rhythms.

CLASSIFICATION (VISUAL, AUDITORY, TACTILE)

footprints and tracks
texture boards
various buttons
patterned popsicle sticks
language phrases
animal/nature sounds

SERIATION

light to dark (skin-colour shades, other colours)
slow to fast
first to last
young to old
1 to 5 Braille dots

COMPARISON (VISUAL, AUDITORY, MOTOR, OLFACTORY)

fabric patterns
script cards
smelly jars
clapping rhythms
pitch and tempo of musical instruments
sign language
walking on crutches, stilts, and snowshoes

DIAGRAM 4.2

DEVELOPMENTAL-BASED WEBBING

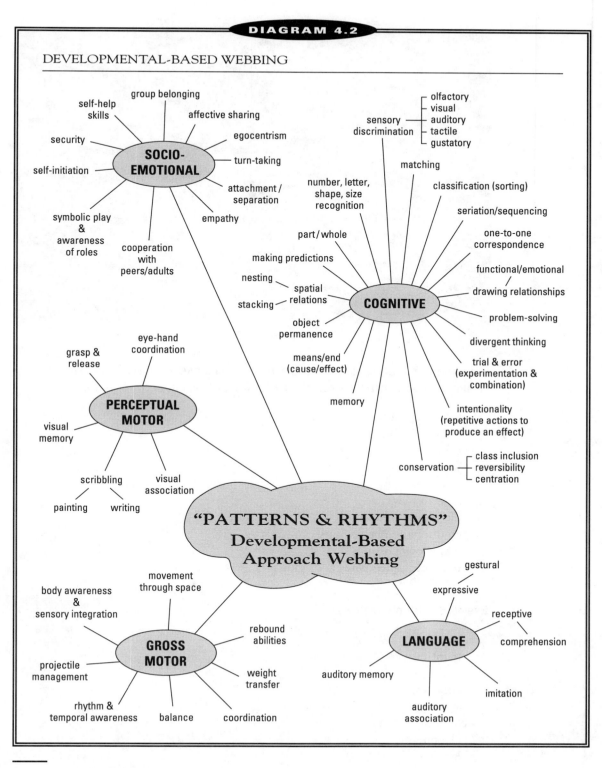

Source: Hall and Rhomberg.

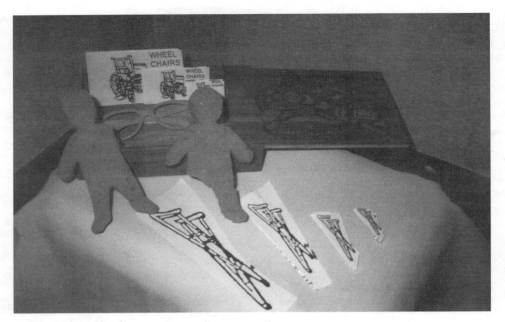

Seriation takes many forms.

Relational Thinking (observation, hypothesis, part/whole, cause/effect, temporal and spatial relations, trial and error, problem-solving)

food preparation and tasting
planting and growth cycle
experiments with water, ice, and temperature
washing and drying clothes
water play
shadow play
blending colours
emotions and behaviours
family composition
life cycle—pregnancy and aging process

Eye-hand Coordination

beading
painting
weaving
collaging
signing
folding
clapping
lacing
drawing

Books, books, and more books.

Communicating in diverse ways

RECEPTIVE AND EXPRESSIVE LANGUAGE (AUDITORY MEMORY, COMPREHENSION, PROBLEM-SOLVING, SEQUENCING, LISTENING TO OTHERS)

> riddles
> chants in various languages
> rhymes and poems
> books with repetitive patterns
> songs in different languages and patterns
> word games
> felt board stories

PROGRAMMING AND ANTI-BIAS SKILLS

The two curriculum approaches both contain opportunities to bring anti-bias skills into the child's daily experiences through:

- exposure to new experiences
- increasing awareness of and comfort with diversity in relation to race, culture, gender, age, and ability
- listening to others
- promoting an enquiring attitude
- drawing relationships between self, others, and family
- building empathy
- providing opportunities for critical thinking
- enabling children to challenge stereotypes.

The final stage in the planning process is selection of appropriate materials and strategies for implementation. The anti-bias approach comes to the fore as children interact with materials. The facilitation by the teacher, which includes posing open-ended questions, anticipating comments, and providing explanation and extensions to children's thinking, challenge children to become more aware of the diversity around them.

The following set of activities illustrates how the anti-bias skills can be incorporated.

1. ACTIVITY: HAIR BEADING ON PEOPLE CARDS

Developmental skills: Eye-hand coordination and sequencing beads to create a pattern.

Anti-bias skills: To foster awareness of racial differences; promote positive self-identity; challenge stereotypes.

Procedure: Cut out large-size pictures of children or adults of different racial backgrounds from magazines. Laminate and glue onto bristol board. Punch out four holes around the head area and knot shoelaces in the back. Provide children with an assortment of beads in individual trays. Both boys and girls can bead the laces in any fashion (older preschoolers can create patterns), and create beaded hair braids on the pictures.

This activity promotes interaction with materials that allows children to explore racial differences while simultaneously challenging the stereotype that only girls play at hairdressing or make "jewellery."

Source: Ofelia Nema, Mothercraft student, 1994.

2. ACTIVITY: EMOTIONS CUBE

Developmental skills: To learn to identify range of emotions; to hypothesize what causes people to feel anger, sadness, joy, frustration, etc.

Anti-bias skills: To listen to others; to value the importance of individual feelings, and build empathy; to challenge statements of discrimination.

Procedure: Acrylic photograph cube or wooden block with pictures of children and adults representing different racial and cultural backgrounds, ages, abilities, and gender. Each picture depicts a different emotion. Each child rolls or tosses the cube. Whatever picture lands face up is the one the child tries to (1) guess what the person is feeling, and (2) express his or her ideas on possible causes. Teachers can facilitate the exploration of anti-bias skills by asking questions that set out situations of discrimination.

Example: "This boy was just called 'fat and ugly' because he wears glasses. How do you think he is feeling? What do you think he should answer?"

3. ACTIVITY: SAND PAINTING

Developmental skills: Eye-hand coordination with manipulation of tool; creativity of design and use of colour; playing with symbols.

Anti-bias skills: to have children try a new experience; to learn about creative expression in a different culture.

Procedure: Show school-age children pictures of artwork from different native peoples (primary images are of animals and people), e.g., Haida, Tlingit, and Tshimshian artists from the Northwest Coast, Inuit from Cape Dorset and Baker Lake, Ojibway and Micmac from the Northeast, and Sioux, Hopi, and Iroquois from the United States. Point out that artists paint certain symbols to tell a story. Introduce the word symbol, show examples, and relate a brief story.

Hold up an example of an aboriginal sand painting which is composed primarily of dots and lines to depict symbols of family gatherings, hunting, the land, and important celebrations. Let children experiment with creating their own symbols and stories using paints and small wooden chopsticks with rounded ends, bamboo skewers without sharp tips, or sticks they have found outside.

(Authors' note: One of the authors travelled extensively throughout the South Pacific when her children were four and eight years old. The children spontaneously tried to recreate the techniques of sand painting after visiting art galleries in Australia's Northern Territory and listening to aboriginal artists tell stories about their paintings. It became a favourite pastime and they grew to appreciate the differences in creative expression among all the peoples in the South Pacific.)

Almost any experience in the life of a young child can work toward promoting the developmental goals and skills of the anti-bias approach, once this educational perspective becomes an engrained way of being and thinking for teachers. It is the authors' hope that teachers will eventually have the same instinctive facility nurturing anti-bias skills that they demonstrate today with those of self-esteem and creativity.

WORKING IT THROUGH

This exercise provides practice in developing activities across the domains using either the developmental-based or theme-based approach.

Identify developmental skill areas or thematic webbed strands and generate five activities for each. Indicate what anti-bias skills each activity promotes (see Chapter 3) and how you would implement them.

Sample:

 Developmental-Based Plan

Developmental Skill Area: Tactile Discrimination

Activity: Braille Placemats

Each child will learn to recognize the composition of Braille dots that represents his/her name. They will design their own placemats making the required dot configuration.

Anti-Bias Skills:

1) awareness and respect for differences in ability

2) ability to try new experience

3) ability to develop empathy

Spatial Relations—

Seriation—

Classification—

Object Permanence—

Imitation—

Part/Whole—

Cause and Effect—

❷ Theme-Based Plan:

Webbed Strands for Life Cycle:

List activities and organize into content areas.

CHAPTER 5

Curriculum Design for Infants and Toddlers

PURPOSE

- *To examine the components of infant curriculum that provide the foundation for the anti-bias approach*

STRATEGIES

- *To explore the dimension of webbing for this age group*
- *To identify how the anti-bias goals support the developmental approach of infant program planning*

MAKING THE CONNECTION

- *Understanding the distinctiveness of infant/toddler curriculum programming*
- *Consolidating the anti-bias approach within infancy and toddlerhood*

The Affective Curriculum

Curriculum planning for infants and toddlers, more so than for any other age, is *relationship based.* By definition curriculum for infants is a dynamic, spontaneous, interactional system (Hall and Flint, 1991), which is constructed through the give-and-take responses that occur between the adult, the infant, and the immediate environment (physical and social). Within this philosophical approach, infant curriculum is neither a box full of prescribed "activities" nor a concentrated effort to "teach" preschool concepts such as size, shapes, colours, and numbers. The core of the curriculum revolves around building relationships and developing attunement to emotional needs. The daily experiences in the lives of infants and toddlers serve as curriculum opportunities (Hall, 1993). By its very nature, this curriculum is an affective one that provides the foundation for the anti-bias approach.

ISSUE OF APPROACH

The dilemma for most early childhood educators who work with this very young age group is that they must cast off the glamorous image of "teacher" and accept the less alluring role of "facilitator." This latter position demands a very different responsibility—one that guides and supports the infant and toddler through the stressful and complex developmental processes. The job of the facilitator involves a dual focus—observing and responding. As the skills of interpreting and analyzing infant/toddler behaviour are challenged again and again, so too grows the expectation of the development of the ability to respond to such cues in a consistent manner that validates and extends a child's experience. The element of program planning is relegated to a much less important position in comparison with the significance of caregiving routines and support of infant mental health.

In light of the previous discussion on curriculum design, it becomes clear that theme-based planning for infants and toddlers provides "artificial and potentially meaningful experiences out of context, so that they have little meaning to the child. A care-giver talks about emotions when emotions occur, not because it is Tuesday of the week of the Emotions theme!" (Stonehouse, 1990, 17). The danger of a theme-based approach is the inability to really focus on what is important to infants and toddlers, so flexibility and spontaneity are sacrificed in the name of more didactic learning.

WEBBING

Webbing for infant/toddler programs must take on a totally different guise than that for older children. Emphasis is placed on key developmental characteristics. The emotional domain, in particular, has areas that should be considered "strands" in the daily program. For example, for infants, self-initiation and sense of agency (being the cause of an action occurring) must be present continuously and repeatedly in the types of play materials offered and in the way social interactions are handled. Infants need many opportunities to demonstrate initiative and agency in order to acquire a positive sense of self. All attempts should be praised and encouraged.

Involving infants in what interests them.

For toddlers, the strands of attachment and separation can be practised in several ways, e.g., endless variations of search-and-find games. Toddlers must have the opportunity not only to find things but to make them disappear as well. Learning that they have some control over an object's appearance and disappearance is essential to a toddler's emerging sense as a separate individual. The use of sensory materials makes the experiences even more enjoyable!

The support of feelings of attachment with the family can be fostered through the use of pretend play with telephones, listening to songs and stories taped by family members, carrying around and looking at notes written by parents whenever the need arises, or cuddling up in a soft, private spot with a personal book of family photos.

The webbing for infant and toddler programs is illustrated in Diagram 5.1.

Supporting feelings of attachment.

DIAGRAM 5.1

WEBBING FOR INFANTS AND TODDLERS

COGNITIVE

Seriation

Classification

Object permanence

Problem-solving

Imitation

Memory

Drawing relationships

Cause and effect

Means/end

LANGUAGE

Receptive language

Expressive language

Visual discrimination

Auditory discrimination

Tactile discrimination

Developmental Approach

SENSORY MOTOR

Sensory manipulation

Trial and error

Experimentation

Eye-hand coordination

Targeting

Visually directed reaching

Visual, auditory, tactile, gustatory, olfactory stimulation

Gross-motor coordination and body awareness

Projectile management and movement

EMOTIONAL

Attachment

Separation

Curiosity

Self-initiation

Sense of agency

Security

Symbolic play

Source: Nadia Hall.

Linking Infant/Toddler Curriculum Design to the Anti-Bias Approach

When we look back to the developmental goals defined by Louise Derman-Sparks in Chapter 3, it becomes clear that the anti-bias approach has its roots in the infancy period. Brazelton first termed the notion of "person creating" (1974) when identifying the primary task of the infant and toddler years. Therefore, the first goal of the anti-bias approach—the construction of a confident, positive self-identity—is well grounded philosophically, theoretically, and developmentally.

GOAL 1: UNDERSTANDING THE CHILD

The nurturing of a child's sense of well-being is all-consuming work for the facilitators. The respect for individual differences commences at the initial parent-teacher interview. Gathering information about sleep routines, handling preferences, eating habits, likes and dislikes of play materials, and developmental abilities is only the starting point. The more essential pieces of information that should be obtained, both from family input and observation, are found in identifying the following:

- styles of relating
- temperamental characteristics
- strategies used to cope with stress
- kinds of experiences and responses to separation
- quality of attachment with the primary care givers

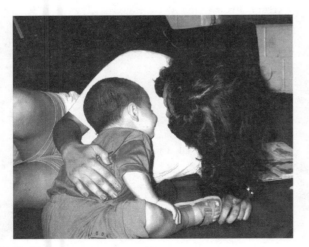

Building a trusting relationship.

For an infant/toddler to feel fully accepted as an individual, each aspect of the child's being must be valued. Facilitators demonstrate such affirmation by creating an environment which supports intimacy, connectedness, and the building of a trusting relationship. The message conveyed to each child is, "I know what you need, want, fear, with or without the ability to express yourself verbally. I will ensure your 'psychological safety' by responding to you in the special way that is yours and yours alone" (Katz, 1983).

Without careful and sensitive attention to these individual emotional needs in infancy, the fate of self-assured, independent, and competent preschoolers is in jeopardy; so too is the basis of the anti-bias approach.

GOAL 2 : INTERACTIONS—BUILDING THE BRIDGES

The second developmental goal, which focuses on building children's comfort with diversity, also has its origins in the infant/toddler years. Exposure to and respect for differences, whether they are related to gender, race, culture, or ability, is as fundamental to the development as the individual differences addressed earlier. When a positive attitude toward differences is communicated naturally, through the course of daily experiences, then children will learn to interact with diversity comfortably. Through the anti-bias approach, children will come to understand that in addition to the many similarities they share, they must also become acquainted with the differences in the human experience.

Facilitators must be in touch with their own values and attitudes because so much of what is communicated to infants and toddlers is through physical contact and social interaction. A hug, a stroke of the hair, a smile, a special look, a nod of the head, the way a child is held, the proximity of the adult, eye contact, or lack of these social exchanges, sends powerful messages to the very young child and affects the child's self-perception.

Self-esteem through sensitive, responsive interactions.

THE MESSAGES WE GIVE

As facilitators we need to ask ourselves the following questions:

- Do we smile more with children of a particular race or gender?
- Do we support curiosity, exploration, and independence equally?
- Do we hold and cuddle certain children differently?
- Do we talk to certain parents with more enthusiasm and purpose than others?
- If we disagree with a family's perspective on child rearing, does that intolerance mirror itself in the way we relate to the child?

- Do we make the attempt to learn the correct pronunciation of all our children's and families' names?

PHYSICAL AND SOCIAL INTERACTIONS

The anti-bias approach with infants and toddlers is primarily conveyed through physical and social interactions. It can manifest itself naturally through thoughtful environmental design and language exchanges, such as:

Supporting curiosity and exploration through close physical interaction.

- exposure to materials that display inclusiveness (dolls, puzzles, books, posters, dramatic play props);
- textures, patterns, and music that reflect a wider, global orientation;
- labelling emotions and feelings appropriate to the situation;
- identifying and discussing differences that are beginning to be discriminated (gender, skin colour, physical attributes);
- songs and finger plays in languages that are culturally representative of families, staff, and the larger community; and
- using opportunities as they arise to make children aware that it is important to listen to the feelings of others, and be open to other points of view.

In the final analysis, for the anti-bias approach to take root, children, at significant developmental stages of their lives, need to have relationships with adults who are willing to take stands about things that are worth doing, worth knowing, and worth caring about (Katz, 1983, 353).

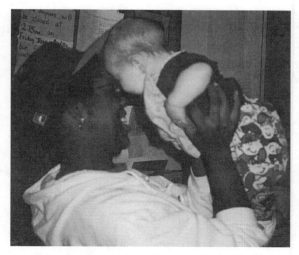

Creating a significant relationship takes time and effort.

CHAPTER 6

Preparation for Designing Anti-Bias Activities

PURPOSE

• *To enable the practitioner to understand how the personal and physical environments in an early childhood setting interact to support the anti-bias goals*

STRATEGIES

• *Three approaches to designing anti-bias activities:*
   1) Incorporation
   2) Personalization
   3) Extension
• *Techniques to facilitate anti-bias skills in activities*
• *Explanation of activity format*

MAKING THE CONNECTION

• *To understand the progression of affective abilities, which enables anti-bias skills to be practised*

The Anti-Bias Approach

The challenge of implementing anti-bias experiences with very young children is to address issues that emerge spontaneously with ease and matter-of-factness. There is never a prepared script that a teacher can follow. Children's remarks or perceptions are markedly individualistic and reflect different developmental levels and concerns. Teachers need to be in a state of readiness to answer questions appropriately, clarify overheard misconceptions, challenge distorted and stereotypic thinking, and build into all the children's relationships an appreciation for individual differences. Children need to know that their curiosity and questions about skin colour, language abilities, or gender, for example, are welcomed. They must hear, see, and feel that they are valued as unique human beings.

Where to Begin—Personal and Physical Environments

A new understanding of developmental appropriateness must take into account not only the lives of children and their development but also the lives of adults. Both teachers and families, as well as the cultural/societal contexts in which we live, should be considered. Where to begin can be relatively easy if the following factors are taken into consideration:

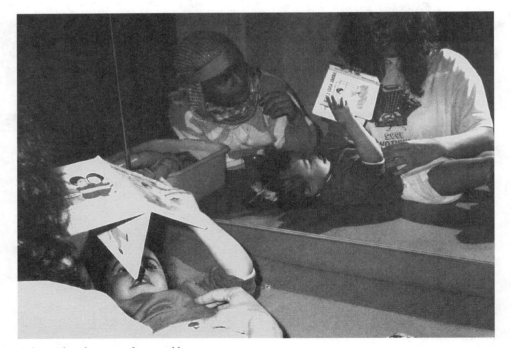

Relationships begin on change tables.

Family reflections in the physical environment.

- the composition of the children in the group
- the composition of the children's families
- the composition of the staff
- the communities of the children and their families
- the global community

The personal environment ensures verbal interactions that promote understanding of self and others in an atmosphere of trust, respect, and acceptance. The role of the adult becomes that of a facilitator. Adult-to-child or child-to-child interactions should be monitored for content and motivation. Not all exclusionary statements are prejudicial or discriminatory in nature. Children may not want to play with one another for a variety of reasons that are acceptable. Teachers should be careful not to make assumptions too quickly about behaviours or statements, but rather explore children's feelings for clarification.

Observations of children's interactions and responses to objects in the physical environment should be carefully assessed as well. The teacher's role is to facilitate the children's comfort levels with objects or experiences that are different or new. When negative remarks or obvious dislikes of differences are demonstrated by children, they need to be addressed. Teachers can capitalize on such opportunities to expand children's thinking regarding diversity.

A discussion held with ECE practitioners around this topic documented just such an opportunity. A teacher in an upper-class white neighbourhood bought multiracial figures to go along with the white ones that came with a doll house. In their play with the new objects, the children began to sort the white figures into separate groups from the multiracial ones. In addition, they assigned the figures

Becoming aware of racial differences.

Valuing diverse cultures.

roles: all the white ones were mommies and daddies, while all the others became nannies and gardeners. What could be perceived as prejudicial behaviours were in fact children practising developmentally appropriate skills of sorting and classifying based on the only experiences they knew. The children had nannies who were Asian and had seen gardeners who were black. They had never encountered black mothers. Due to their limited exposure, the children were unintentionally stereotyping people along racial lines. The teacher realized that she needed to clarify the children's perceptions and provide correct information. This was done through posing divergent questions such as, "Do you think nannies can be mommies? Do you think *all* nannies look like this?" and following up by reading several books that portray people of different racial backgrounds in diverse roles. These strategies eventually helped the children realize that people of all backgrounds can be a mommy, a gardener, or a nanny. This situation demonstrates the potential consequences of excluding multiracial figures from the physical environment or of committing the equally grave error of **tokenism**. In this case, the figures acted as a catalyst in surfacing children's misconceptions, and afforded the teacher an opportunity for extensive dialogue and critical thinking.

The inclusion of items in the physical environment that reflect the children, the families, and the staff, will quite naturally incorporate the many cultural and societal diversities inherent in the program. If the composition of the group is homogeneous, it becomes crucial to include items representing humanity's differences in order to prepare the children for interacting with the diversity that will be a reality in their lives. Items that can be obtained from families and friends, or that can be made inexpensively, become the learning environment for both teachers and children. These materials serve as stimuli for inquiry and experimentation, and they ultimately lead to a clearer knowledge of the value and belief systems influencing the relationships in the group.

For further suggestions on how to create a welcoming physical environment, see the charts in the Appendix, pages 193–97.

Activity Approaches

When attempting implementation of anti-bias activities, three approaches are possible: (1) incorporation, (2) personalization, and (3) extension (Rhomberg, 1993).

INCORPORATION

This approach works well with all age groups. It entails including an item which clearly reflects one or more areas of bias into the activity preparation. For example, water play can include sponges in a variety of people shapes (such as tall, small, fat, armless, legless, skinny); equipment for children who are physically challenged; homes; transportation modes, as well as various shades of skin tones. The variety of sponges exposes children to the relevant areas of appearance, ability, class, and race. To enhance exposure to additional areas, pictures of different family compositions, of males and females in nonstereotypical activities (gender), or of young and old people enjoying similar activities (age), could be attached either to the water table itself or displayed in the water-play area. By adding a spice (such as curry or cumin) or a utensil from a different cultural group, yet another area of bias, culture, has been incorporated.

Incorporation of anti-bias materials in sensory play.

The developmental capabilities of children must always be primary when using the incorporation approach. It would be inappropriate and irrelevant to include most of the items mentioned above in an activity geared to infants as they are incapable of multidimensional thinking. For infants, the inclusion of a utensil for motor-coordination practice and a spice for gustatory/olfactory stimulation satisfies both developmental challenges and anti-bias skill building.

PERSONALIZATION

The personalization approach depends upon a "real person," representing an area of diversity, visiting and interacting with the children. Visitors are invited to participate in a program's range of activities. Caution must be exercised, however, to avoid stereotyping the guest by focusing only on certain activities. Ideally, a person in a wheelchair, for example, would be present on more than one occasion and would engage in many different activities with the children rather than just passive ones, such as reading and singing.

This approach allows the children an opportunity to interact closely with someone whom society designates as different. Each age group will benefit in various ways. The toddler gains exposure; the preschooler may have stereotypes dispelled; and the school-age child may be moved to become pro-active within his own environment. The personalization approach is a concrete strategy to introduce and make familiar the varied areas of bias.

EXTENSION

The extension approach lends itself more successfully with preschool and school-age children. Any activity can be extended into one or more areas of bias through appropriate **divergent questions**. For example, an art activity in which children are using their hands to hold brushes and paint can be extended into the "ability" area through the following strategy: "I see you are using both your hands to paint. Do you think someone who has no arms is able to paint with a brush?"

The children's answers will provide not only insight into their thinking but also may provide an opportunity to hear misconceptions, fears, and other emotional perspectives on this issue. Following up their comments with another open-ended question such as, "How many different ways do you think someone who has no arms can pick up their brush?" provides an opportunity for problem-solving and critical thinking.

When the children's suggestions are taken seriously and an encouraging "let's try it" attitude overrides the agenda of the activity, the seed to understanding what it may feel like to be a person without arms has been planted. The germination of the anti-bias skill of empathy, however, needs continual nourishment. The outcome of such an extension can have two different results, depending on the ages of the children. An older preschooler might experience a moment of true empathy; a school-age child might take up a plan for action that arose from the processes of critical thinking and problem-solving.

A child's affective development is enriched when her feelings of self-worth and self-esteem increase as a result of actively bringing about positive change on behalf of someone else. These feelings of empowerment are the building blocks toward future pro-activism—the end goal of the anti-bias approach to working with young children.

The Affective Progression— Exposure, Familiarity, Comfort, Empathy, Pro-Activism

Children need both time and opportunity to learn how to express feelings (see Diagram 6.1). If children are to become pro-active and able to stand up for themselves and others in the face of inequity, the process of affective development needs to begin in infancy.

The infancy period provides a natural starting point. Everything and everyone is new to the infant and will be explored with curiosity. Exposure to objects and people that reflect diversity turns what might otherwise be perceived as extraordinary experiences into ordinary events. The toddler who continues to be exposed to differences cannot help but acquire a familiarity and comfort level with diversity. However, it is not until a child enters the preschool years that primitive expressions of empathy may be demonstrated, if adults provide carefully guided interactions. True empathy can only emerge when children are able to understand how being different actually feels. This affective task requires moving beyond egocentrism—a feat that the school-age child should be able to achieve.

The final step in the progression of affective development in the anti-bias approach is the ability to challenge discrimination in concrete ways on behalf of one's self and others. The adult is instrumental in the development of the pro-active child. Children's energies need to be focused and supported as they organize actions in the name of a particular cause.

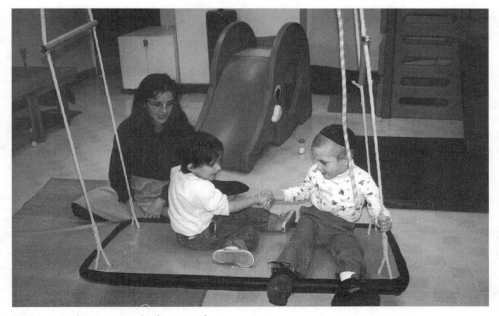

Positive social interactions lead to empathy.

DIAGRAM 6.1

AFFECTIVE PROGRESSION

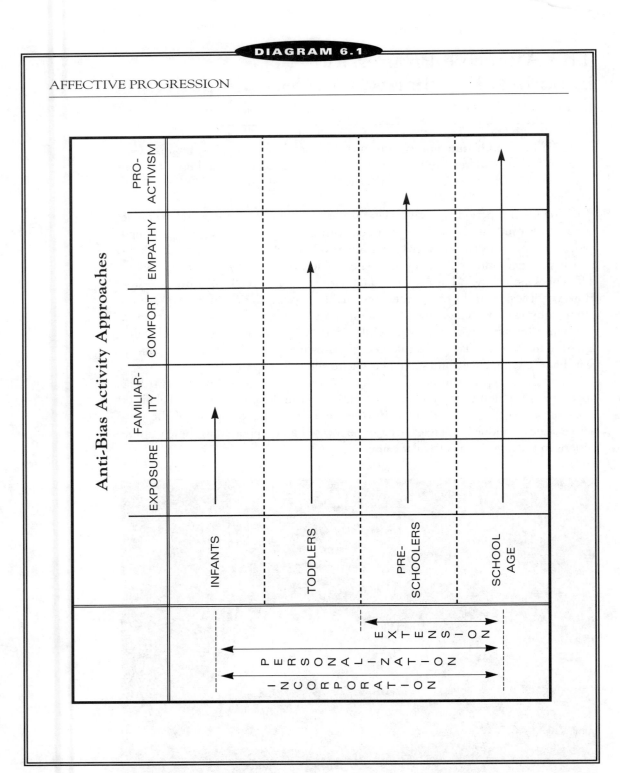

Source: Hall and Rhomberg.

A journal entry by a student in early childhood education clearly illustrates how repeated exposure to a new experience can make the extraordinary ordinary and can assist children to interact with diversity comfortably. The student was Muslim and always wore the *hijab* (scarf head covering) in class and on field placement. Four weeks into her placement with preschoolers, she decorated the "travel agency" dramatic play area with numerous pictures of people and places from around the world. A group of four-year-olds questioned and commented extensively on several photographs. Included among the pictures was one of young Malaysian girls in hijabs. The student writes:

> The children looked at the picture but made no comment which was unusual because they had commented on all the others. I was rather pleased by this because it showed an awareness and acceptance of women in "hijab." I know that my wearing one was a new experience for the children, given their initial questions about it. The fact that they did not comment on the picture shows that exposure to a woman in hijab gave them the *concrete* exposure for it (the hijab) to become secondary to their interaction and consideration of that person. (Ayesha Mondal, Mothercraft student, 1994)

This example serves to demonstrate how facilitation of materials meets a central goal of the anti-bias approach. Children who have an attitude of enquiry and openness to new experiences instilled from early on approach differences in a non-judgmental fashion. Teachers need to allow children to explore their own identity safely, as they compare their own characteristics and abilities with those they see in others. In this way children who feel self-assured will be more able to accept diversity in its many appearances.

It is only through thoughtful and sensitive preparation of the physical and personal environment that competing values can find a peaceful co-existence.

Given that teachers can never be totally prepared when they overhear discriminatory remarks, the following scenarios are provided as examples of possible scripts, with indications of how issues can be handled appropriately and inappropriately. The most significant of all the strategies is the *immediate response*, no matter how difficult to do the teacher may find this.

SCENARIO 1: HEIDI COMES HOME FROM KINDERGARTEN AND SAYS TO HER MOTHER: "JULIA TOLD ME THAT OUR FAMILY IS WEIRD. SHE SAID I HAVE TWO MOMMIES AND I'M SUPPOSED TO HAVE A MOMMY AND A DADDY. WHAT'S WRONG WITH OUR FAMILY, MOMMY?"

Answer A: "Don't pay attention to Julia. She doesn't know what a family is all about."

Answer B: "Are you confused/upset by what Julia said? There's nothing wrong with our family. There are many different ways of being a family. In our family we have a mommy and a mommy. Who else do you think could be in a family? Can you think of some of your other friends and who are in their families?"

Answer C: "Those people are always saying mean things. Keep out of her way."

If you selected A, you were using the **dismissal technique** and wanted to avoid any tension involved with the issue. If you selected B, you used a range of strategies which included: reflecting feelings; providing accurate information; addressing feelings that were inappropriate to the situation; problem-solving and building empathy. If you selected C, you were using an overgeneralization to put down the other child's remark. This effectively closes any possible dialogue on the comment.

SCENARIO 2: AT GROUP TIME A TEACHER IS READING THE BOOK *HOW MY PARENTS LEARNED TO EAT* TO THE CHILDREN. SUDDENLY TOMMY PIPES UP, "MICHAEL SAYS ALL PAKIS SMELL."

Answer A: "When you call people names it upsets me. People who come from Pakistan have names, just like you and me. Remember when we had the smelly jars at the science table—and you smelled the ginger, cumin, and cloves? They all smelled differently, didn't they?"

Answer B: Teacher does not respond and continues to read.

Answer C: "They all smell like that because they use those spices."

If you selected A, you responded immediately to the racist remark by clearly expressing your disapproval of it, and by providing accurate information. If you selected B, you elected to ignore the racist remark, which conveys tacit approval. If you selected C, you engaged in negative stereotyping which contributes to the already biased perspective the child holds.

SCENARIO 3 : ONE NINE-YEAR-OLD CHILD SAYS TO ANOTHER: "DON'T TOUCH OUR PROJECT WITH YOUR DIRTY BLACK HANDS."

Answer A: "What is it about Darren's hands that upset you?"

Answer B: "Do you understand that what you just said makes Darren feel that he is not as good as you? This is a racist statement. In this classroom, everyone, no matter what skin colour he has, has the right to touch, play, or look at the materials." To the rest of the group, "So when you hear remarks like that, what do you think we should be answering?"

Answer C: "I don't think you really meant to say that to Darren. What do we say in our classroom when we don't want people touching our things?"

If you selected A, you were simply clarifying the remark by reflecting the child's feelings. This is a good start, but you should have confronted the issue as well. If you selected B, you addressed the issue of racism squarely and encouraged the group to engage in pro-active problem-solving around answering such remarks. If you selected C, you deflected the racial remark by refocusing on the issue of manners. This type of redirection avoids dealing with the conflict.

SCENARIO 4: YOU ARE A TEACHER SUPERVISING ON THE PLAYGROUND AND YOU SEE A GRADE 5 STUDENT WALKING UP TO TWO CHILDREN. HE PROCEEDS TO SAY, "YOU'RE A JEW AND YOU'RE A JEW. I'M HITLER. WATCH OUT 'CAUSE I'M GOING TO GET YOU."

Answer A: "Jimmy, why are you saying this to David and Leon? It's not very nice when you insult people like that."

Answer B: "Don't say things like that in a public place."

Answer C: "I will not have you threaten anyone because of who they are. What Hitler did was very wrong. We call it racism because he believed that Jewish people were less human than others."

If you selected A, you were offering a mild protest in a generalized manner. There is neither a challenge nor an explanation offered in response to the discriminatory remark. If you selected B, you decided to avoid the conflict by using the place as an excuse for keeping silent. The implication of the answer is that it is acceptable to make such remarks behind closed doors. If you selected C, you took a firm stand against a racist remark and voiced your intolerance at its utterance.

There are three key questions to consider when overhearing a racist or discriminatory remark:

1. How is the racism being expressed?

2. How would you help the child to understand the implications of the statement and to learn that such an attitude is hurtful?

3. What follow-up action would you take?

The activities that follow in the next four chapters are not meant to be prescriptive but were designed to demonstrate the following:

1. Anti-bias elements can be infused naturally into any key experience with children, irrespective of content or developmental areas. This does not mean that teachers plan "to do Braille on Monday and wheelchairs on Tuesday. That way children can group those who can walk and those who can't." The focus must always be positive, i.e., "We all can move around, how we do it may be different (e.g., trike, car, wheelchair, wagon, bus, skates)." An area of diversity should be treated as one of many aspects for the children to think about rather than an example given in isolation.

2. The anti-bias approach can only make a difference if materials are supported with sensitive and developmentally relevant facilitation.

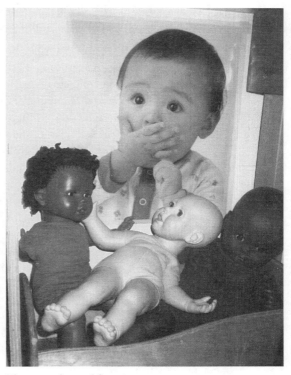

The many faces of diversity.

Activity Format— Explanation of Key Terms

Curriculum area: This term refers to the selected area of focus of a child's development.

Curriculum objectives: These objectives reflect the primary skills that will be practised. They must flow directly from the curriculum area; for example, if the curriculum area is language, the overriding purpose is to design activities that will develop language skills such as listening, identifying, labelling, describing, and so on.

Developmental skills: Given the holistic orientation of the anti-bias approach, this section contains pertinent skills that can be selected from the remaining developmental domains (i.e., cognitive, affective, and motor).

Anti-bias skills: The skills identified in this section assist children in practising the four major goals outlined in Chapter 3 and support teachers and children in their interaction with diversity. Selection of these skills needs to be carefully considered in relation to developmental capabilities.

Level: This section describes how materials can be categorized when moving children from a concrete to an abstract experience.

The term *concrete* identifies materials that are hands on and manipulative.

The term *representational*, for the sole purpose of these activities, refers to two-dimensional items such as pictures, books, and photos.

The term *symbolic* designates abstract materials such as printed words, numbers, and any other symbol linked to literacy.

The majority of materials in the Infant Activity chapter, of developmental necessity, are concrete. As the child's cognitive abilities mature, introduction of more representational and symbolic materials becomes apparent. However, a good balance of all three levels should be maintained as a child enters the school-age years.

Facilitation: This section attempts to show how activities can be implemented in order to meet the stated curriculum objectives and anti-bias skills.

Focus: This section explains the procedure and clearly indicates how the curriculum objectives can be achieved.

Comments: This section presents the actual verbal strategies that emphasize the stated anti-bias skills. Verbal strategies can consist of either statements or divergent questions.

The use of divergent questions is developmentally limited to preschoolers and school-age children. Some examples to facilitate critical thinking about diversity can include:

How else do you think you can …? (preschool)
How many different ways can you …? (school age)

Why do you think ...? (both ages)

What do you think would happen if ...? (both ages)

Variation or extension: Some activities can exercise the same skills using different materials as a variation on a theme. Other activities have a natural follow-up to extend the learning and skill practice. However, not all activities that are presented here include a variation or an extension section.

WORKING IT THROUGH

Complete the following chart. For each activity, identify:

1) the anti-bias goal

2) the anti-bias area

3) the approach

The first activity has been completed as an example.

An additional exercise for practice would be to borrow program plans from local child-care centres or lab-school centres and modify existing activities for the required anti-bias elements outlined in the chart.

PROMOTING AWARENESS OF DIVERSITY IN CHILDREN					
ACTIVITY	**CURRICULUM AREA**	**ANTI-BIAS AREA**	**APPROACH**	**AGE OF CHILD**	**GOAL**
water play with sponges in various human shapes (fat, small, legless, armless), skin-tone paint ("people" colour) added to water, curry added to water	socio-emotional	appearance ability race culture	incorporation	infant toddler preschool	building self-identity
invite a person in a wheel-chair to join in finger-painting. Use "people" paint on laminated pictures depicting older persons, children, and adults from many cultural backgrounds	sensory/ creative			infant toddler preschool	
walk with crutches; walk, skip, hop—blindfolded or without use of arms, or with one leg only	gross motor			preschool	
puzzles depicting women and men of diverse races in non-traditional roles	cognitive			toddlers preschool	
read book such as *Horace,* where the main character suffers from discriminatory behaviours; problem-solve actions to take in present situation and in others, i.e., if Horace were blind; create own story	language			preschool school-age	

CHART 6.1

Source: Hall and Rhomberg.

CHAPTER 7

Developmental-Based Infant Activities within an Anti-Bias Framework

PURPOSE

• To enable the practitioner to explore the range of activities appropriate for infants within an anti-bias framework

STRATEGIES

• Designed and formatted activities that include anti-bias skills for each developmental domain for ages 3–18 months
• Explanation of the interaction process found in the "facilitation" portion of each activity
• Suggested implementation techniques to convey the anti-bias approach

MAKING THE CONNECTION

• To understand through the presentation of a completed weekly program plan, with anti-bias sections, how children can:
  1) practise anti-bias skills on a daily basis
  2) be exposed to each area of bias at least once a week

Activities for Infants

The expectation of implementing an anti-bias approach for teachers working with infants is developmentally compatible with responsive caregiving. The fostering of a strong sense of self is the major task in the affective domain. Adults convey powerful messages of acceptance or intolerance in the ways they interact with infants.

Babies are aware of and able to interpret adult responses to people and objects. Verbal comments, voice inflection, facial expressions, gestures, and body posture can all signal either respect or disrespect in an infant's social environment. Appropriate adult modelling lays the foundation for a positive self-image as infants begin to feel valued for who they are, who their families are, and who others in their lives are.

The anti-bias approach with infants begins with exposure to differences in people and objects. The infants, through sensorimotor exploration of people and toys will start to build an understanding of sense of self and what they can do in relation to others. If the objects and people in an infant's physical environment reflect a representation of diversity, then the infant will acquire familiarity in a natural manner.

Activities with this very young age group need to revolve around building relationships. This occurs when adults support infants' bids for self-initiated play, follow infants' leads, support attempts at problem-solving and, in general, make infants feel good about who they are. For this reason, all of the activities in this chapter are developmentally based.

WEEKLY PLAN					
AGE: INFANT	**SKILL ☑ THEME-RELATED ☐ (✓ BOX)**			**IDENTIFY SKILL/THEME: CAUSE AND EFFECT**	
	Language	**Socioemotional**	**Sensory**	**Motor**	**Remarks**
Monday	Language Block	Mirror Reflections	Cinnamon Mud	Symphony of Pots and Pans	
A-B AREA	Age-race-ability	Gender-race	Race	Culture-gender	
A-B SKILL	Awareness of age and gender	Sense of self	Exposure to new experiences	Differences in cultural utensils	
Tuesday	Scarf Scramble	Moving Faces	Mat Fun	Lazy Susan Patterns	
A-B AREA	Culture	Gender-race	Culture	All areas	
A-B SKILL	Differences in cultural textures	Self-concept	Differences in cultural textures	Exposure to differences	
Wednesday	Action Songs	Board Book of Emotions	Sticky Patterns	Package Wrap	
A-B AREA	Culture	Age-race-abilities	Culture	All areas	
A-B SKILL	Awareness of differences	Self-concept	Differences in cultural patterns	Exposure to differences	
Thursday	Squeeze Play	Family Sounds	Finger Paint Pictures	Peg Releasing	
A-B AREA	Race-culture	Gender-culture	All areas	Age-gender	
A-B SKILL	Promoting sense of self	Recognize value of each family	Promote familiarity	Label feelings	
Friday	Peek-a-Boo Photo Board	Baby Bath Time	Tapioca Taste	Lids and Containers	
A-B AREA	All areas	Gender-race	Race	Culture	
A-B SKILL	Recognize value of each child	Exposure to differences	Exposure to new experience	Similarities/ differences	
Dramatic/Social Play Props		Water Table Play Props		Sand Table Play Props	

Source: Hall and Rhomberg.

ACTIVITY 1   Language Block

▶ **Age:** 6–18 months

▶ **Curriculum Area:** Language (expressive and receptive)

▶ **Curriculum Objectives:** Identify and associate labels with objects

▶ **Developmental Skills:** Memory; fine-motor manipulation; using two hands together; spatial awareness of top and bottom

▶ **Anti-Bias Skill:** To familiarize the infant with people of different races, gender, and ability; to promote a positive sense of self

▶ **Materials:** Large acrylic photograph box with pictures inserted on all six sides. Pictures can be rotated so as to emphasize different concepts, i.e., six babies of different racial backgrounds with six different toys; family photos including children and adults; objects reflecting the child's family environment.

▶ **Level:** Representational

Facilitation

Focus: Encourage the infant to rotate/turn box around and upside down in order to look at all of the pictures. Point to photos as you label them simply. Praise the infant as he finds a photo in response to a label.

Comments/Questions: Look what you found—it's a baby sleeping.

Let's turn it again—what's on the bottom/side?

It's auntie reading a book to a baby.

This looks like your brother. He is spinning a top.

Variation or Extension: Make individual language blocks with photos of the family and pictures of objects that are relevant to each child (any transitional object from home, favourite food, certain objects associated with parents, i.e., glasses, earrings, hat, etc.).

Language blocks.

ACTIVITY 2   Scarf Scramble

▶ *Age:* 12–18 months

▶ *Curriculum Area:* Language

▶ *Curriculum Objectives:* Receptive and expressive language (labelling actions); social interaction

▶ *Developmental Skills:* Eye-hand coordination; imitation; pulling and grasping; visual and tactile discrimination; and object permanence

▶ *Anti-Bias Skill:* Exposure to textures and patterns from other cultures

▶ *Materials:* Variety of scarves (texture, pattern, colour, and size), include some sheer ones; shoe box covered with pictures representative of areas of bias; scissors, wrapping or contact paper. Knot scarves together and place inside a lidded box.

▶ *Level:* Concrete

Facilitation

Focus: Encourage the infant to pull scarves out of the box imitating your action. Play peek-a-boo with the scarves as they are exiting from the hole. Label not only the actions involved but also the colours, patterns, textures, and sizes of the scarves.

Comments: You're pulling the scarf! It's a big scarf.

Peek-a-boo!

Pull more—look, another scarf is coming out.

This scarf has zigzags.

Let's pull some more.

This scarf is silky and smooth.

Variation or Extension: Add spice to the box or dip one end of several of the scarves in a different scent; let dry. Repeat the activity and focus in on the smell (i.e., clove, cumin, rose).

ACTIVITY 3   Action Songs

▶ *Age:* 6–18 months

▶ *Curriculum Area:* Language

▶ *Curriculum Objectives:* To help infants learn actions and spatial relations through rhythm and songs

▶ *Developmental Skills:* Large-muscle coordination; weight shift and balance; building upper- and lower-body strength

▶ *Anti-Bias Skill:* To expose infants to similar actions in different languages

▶ *Materials:* Collect short rhymes and songs in different languages that emphasize moving through space: up and down and around.

▶ *Level:* Concrete

Facilitation

Focus: Encourage the infant to make the connection between words and actions. The level of interactive participation will depend upon the infant's motor skills. For a sitting infant, play out these rhymes on your lap or while supporting the infant to stand and bounce to the words; for walking infants, do the rhyme in pairs. Emphasize the words up, down, around in all languages, particularly those languages that are represented in your group of children and staff.

Comments: Roly-poly, roly-poly (rolling hands)

In-in-in (hands in)

Roly-poly, roly-poly

Out-out-out
Roly-poly, roly-poly
Up-up-up
Roly-poly, roly-poly

Down-down-down

Variation or Extension: For older infants, incorporate signing for up, down, and around into the songs/finger play.

ACTIVITY 4 Squeeze Play

► **Age:** 12–18 months

► **Curriculum Area:** Language

► **Curriculum Objectives:** Visual exploration; receptive language; imitation and repetition

► **Developmental Skills:** Eye-hand coordination in squeezing, releasing, cause and effect

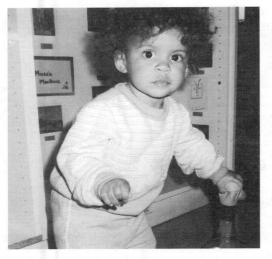

Look what I can do!

► **Anti-Bias Skill:** To promote **sense of agency** (causing something to happen)

► **Materials:** Plastic, transparent container with narrow opening, turkey baster, water, glycerin, sequins, beads and buttons from different cultures, cloth tape (see accompanying photo)

► **Level:** Concrete

Facilitation

Focus: Encourage the infant to imitate as you demonstrate squeezing the bulb of the baster. Focus the infant's attention on the swirling sequins, buttons, or beads as they rise and descend through the water. Help the infant to repeat an action so she can discover that the action produces movement and interesting changes.

Comments: Squeeze it.

Look at the buttons, moon, stars, fish, etc., moving up.

Oh, look, the star is falling down.

The fish is swimming up, up, up.

Do it again.

Source: Activity courtesy of Pamela Jones.

ACTIVITY 5　Peek-a-Boo Photo Board

▶ *Age:* 12–18 months

▶ *Curriculum Area:* Language

▶ *Curriculum Objectives:* To practise visual identification; to express names of peers in the group; to promote positive sense of self and others

▶ *Developmental Skills:* Fine-motor coordination; object permanence; exploration of directionality; trial-and-error experimentation

▶ *Anti-Bias Skill:* To strengthen self-identity and value uniqueness of others

▶ *Materials:* Individual photos of the children mounted on cardboard. Cover the pictures either from the top or from the side with thin Velcro and different types of material, i.e., gauze, net, fabric, crinkly cellophane, etc., or glue cardboard over the photos and cut out doors on three sides so that children can push them open and shut over the photos.

▶ *Level:* Concrete and representational

Facilitation

Focus: Helps infants to explore photos hidden under the cloth/cardboard by engaging them in a hide-and-seek game. Label the child on the photo and describe what he looks like and what

Working on object permanence while developing self-identity.

he is doing. Encourage the infant to engage in trial-and-error experimentation as he lifts the covering from the bottom up, right to left, or left to right direction.

Comments/Questions: Who is under/behind the door?

Oh, look, it's Jaime! What's Jaime doing?
He is holding a baby doll.
Nice hugs.
Who's this? It's Malcolm.

That's you! You have your hat and snowsuit on.

Variation or Extension: Make a family photo album for each child; laminate pictures of children of different racial, cultural backgrounds, gender, or ability, playing, eating, dressing, and tape pictures to the floor. Comment as the infant explores them casually during crawling, stepping, or walking movements.

ACTIVITY 6   Mirror Reflections

▶ **Age:** 6–18 months

▶ **Curriculum Area:** Socioemotional

▶ **Curriculum Objectives:** Positive self-image; body awareness

▶ **Developmental Skills:** Eye-hand coordination; object permanence; sensory pleasure

▶ **Anti-Bias Skill:** To foster a positive sense of self and to value the uniqueness of others

▶ **Materials:** Water bin, coloured water, small plastic mirrors at the bottom of the container

▶ **Level:** Concrete

Facilitation

Focus: Encourage infants during water play to reach in for mirror, peer into water to try to find and feel their image. Reinforce the infant watching what she feels her body doing. Make the connection between body parts and self-identity.

Comments/Questions: Who's that in the water? I see Nicky.

Look, can you touch the mirror?
There's your hand, your mouth.
Where's Nicky?
You dropped the mirror in the water.
Look, I see Jamal. This is Jamal's nose/finger.

Variation or Extension: Provide an assortment of props that have different sized holes, i.e., sieves, colanders, rice paddle, ladles with holes. Focus the infant's attention to how slowly or quickly the water drips, pours, and sprinkles. Label the props from different cultures accurately.

ACTIVITY 7   Moving Faces

▶ **Age:** 6–12 months

▶ **Curriculum Area:** Socioemotional

▶ **Curriculum Objectives:** To help infants recognize facial expressions; to encourage infants to repeat pleasurable actions; to encourage infants to understand that they are the cause of objects moving

▶ **Developmental Skills:** Goal-directed reaching with one arm; receptive language, and visual discrimination

▶ **Anti-Bias Skill:** To foster a positive self-concept and a sense of agency

▶ **Materials:** Small milk cartons covered in fabric and suspended by elastic from a clothes hanger, the ceiling, or a clothesline. Each carton should have a large picture of a child/adult (representing the areas of diversity), with a happy or sad face. Bells, rice, or pebbles can be added to a few of the cartons for incongruity, to provide sound and weight differences.

▶ **Level:** Concrete

Facilitation

Focus: Give the infant an opportunity to practise a variety of motor skills by lowering or raising the cartons so that he can reach, pull, and hit the faces from the sit, crawl, or supine positions. Label the feelings represented on each carton as the infant makes contact. Relate your words to the infant's emotional states.
Comments: Come on, Marisa, stretch, reach for the happy face.
   Good hit/kick! You made the sad face swing.
   Oh, oh, the happy face has a sound. Hear the bell?
   You are smiling just like the daddy!
Variation or Extension: For very young infants, glue unbreakable mirrors on the bottom of cartons so that they can see themselves as they reach for and play with the moving cartons.

ACTIVITY 8   Board Book of Emotions

▶ **Age:** 12–18 months

▶ **Curriculum Area:** Socioemotional

▶ **Curriculum Objectives:** To foster security and a sense of self; to identify simple emotions

▶ **Developmental Skills:** Visual discrimination; receptive language; labelling feelings

▶ **Anti-Bias Skill:** To promote a feeling of self-concept and familiarity with all areas of diversity

▶ **Materials:** Large, clear, simple pictures of adults/children representing a variety of ages, abilities, gender, races, and cultures; contact paper, cardboard, rings/yarn

▶ **Level:** Representational

Facilitation

Focus: Label emotions, people, and actions and relate the feelings to the infant.
Comments: To the picture of a boy in a wheelchair catching a ball: Happy boy, look, he is catching a ball.
   Daddy's feeding the baby, happy baby.
   Angry baby.
   Sad mommy.

Variation or Extension: Ensure that each infant has a book of his or her own family made by the staff and parents. This book should be available to the child at all times and will become a transition tool when the infant moves to the toddler room.

ACTIVITY 9 Family Sounds

▶ **Age:** 3–18 months

▶ **Curriculum Area:** Socioemotional

▶ **Curriculum Objectives:** To establish a sense of family belonging; to foster self-esteem

▶ **Developmental Skills:** Auditory discrimination and tracking; attachment

▶ **Anti-Bias Skill:** To understand the relationship to one's own family and to value the uniqueness of others

▶ **Materials:** Tape recorder and blank tapes

▶ **Level:** Concrete

Facilitation

Focus: Provide the infant with opportunities to listen to familiar sounds of people and objects.

The younger the child, the greater the need for simplicity and clarity of voices and sounds to avoid confusion. Involve parents or other care givers by asking them to tape themselves and their families at various times throughout the day (meals, sleep routines, bath time, etc.). Make sure voices of individual members are speaking or singing in their own language. Play tape(s) to infant(s) on an individual basis or as a group.
Comments: Oh, there's Nouran's mommy singing!

This is Sin-Le's daddy putting the lid on the wok.

I hear Kevin's grandmother laughing.

Listen to the footsteps—oops! They're gone now—up the stairs.
Variation or Extension: Start a collection of songs that represent the favourites of your children and that are taped by their families.

ACTIVITY 10 Baby Bath Time

▶ **Age:** 12–18 months

▶ **Curriculum Area:** Socioemotional

▶ **Curriculum Objectives:** To provide an opportunity for the infant to gain understanding of his own feelings and needs; to promote a sense of self

▶ **Developmental Skills:** Fine-motor manipulation; receptive language related to emotional needs; early symbolic play

▶ **Anti-Bias Skill:** To foster recognition of others' needs; participation in nonstereotypical activity

▶ **Materials:** Multiracial and different gender dolls, wash basin, towels from different cultures, face cloths, various sponges (include sea sponge and different shades of brown, to reflect a variety of skin tones), large empty powder container, plastic/training pants

▶ **Level:** Concrete

Facilitation

Focus: Provide dolls, bathing props, and warm water for the infants to play with. Encourage boys and girls to clean, pat dry, powder, and nurture the dolls.

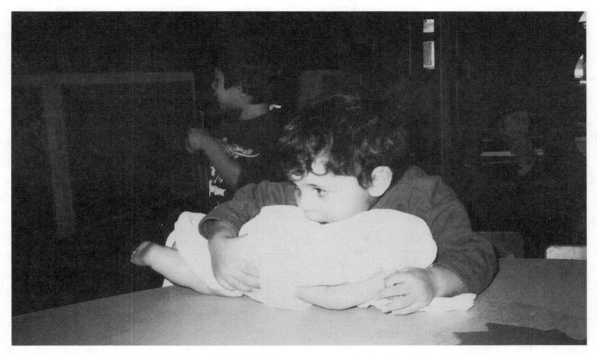

Promotion of anti-stereotypical play in toddlerhood.

Comments/Questions: Is your baby enjoying her bath?
    Wash her hair, legs, tummy, etc.
    Is she all clean?
    Let's dry her and make sure she is warm.

Comment on the nature of the sponges and towels as they are used.

Variation or Extension: Provide a doll with a missing limb, with a leg brace, glasses, etc.

ACTIVITY 11 Cinnamon Mud

▶ *Age:* 6—18 months

▶ *Curriculum Area:* Sensory

▶ *Curriculum Objectives:* Tactile, visual, olfactory, and gustatory exploration

▶ *Developmental Skills:* Acting on sensory materials to produce interesting effects; fine-motor manipulation

▶ *Anti-Bias Skill:* To promote familiarity with smells not usually experienced

▶ *Materials:* "Goop" made with brown paint and cinnamon

▶ *Level:* Concrete

Facilitation

Focus: Encourage the infant to explore sensory material with eyes, hands, mouth, and nose. Label the sensations of smell, taste, and texture as well as the lines, circles, and spaces made during the exploration.

Comments/Questions: Devon, look what's happening to your hands.

Let's look at Roger's hands.

Smell your fingers. Mmm, cinnamon!

Variation or Extension: Add whatever scent or spice to which your group of children would not normally be exposed.

ACTIVITY 12   Mat Fun

▶ **Age:** 6–18 months

▶ **Curriculum Area:** Sensory

▶ **Curriculum Objectives:** Tactile and visual exploration and discrimination

▶ **Development Skills:** Crawling and walking on different surfaces; associating textures and sensations receptively

▶ **Anti-Bias Skill:** To expose infants to patterns and textures from other cultures

▶ **Materials:** Square mats with a variety of textures, e.g., woven, bamboo, shag, cotton, straw, velvet, corduroy

▶ **Level:** Concrete

Facilitation

Focus: Encourage infants to crawl, walk, and explore with bare feet various mats taped to the floor. Allow them to pick, stroke, and scratch textures.

Comments/Questions: What a soft mat; feel the lines on this mat—it is smooth.

This mat is all bumpy.

How does this one feel on your toes?

Is it scratchy?

Continue to comment not only on the tactile dimension but also the visual, i.e., designs, pictures, and colours.

Variation or Extension: Use your floor as another opportunity for exposure to diversity by taping laminated pictures on it that represent age, appearance, abilities, gender, or any other pictures that reflect as many areas of bias possible.

ACTIVITY 13   Sticky Patterns

▶ **Age:** 9–18 months

▶ **Curriculum Area:** Sensory

▶ **Curriculum Objectives:** Tactile and visual exploration of patterns, shapes, and sizes

▶ **Developmental Skills:** Fine-motor coordination in targeting and release; cause and effect; motor practice in weight shifts to other positions; receptive-language labelling of colour, texture, and size

▶ **Anti-Bias Skill:** To expose the infant to patterns and textures from other cultures

▶ **Materials:** Assortment of prints, solids, and patterns cut in various shapes and sizes from burlap, silk, velvet, corduroy, leather, feather, gauze, suede, cotton, etc.; large sheet of contact paper sticky side out, taped onto free wall space no higher than one metre from the floor.

▶ **Level:** Concrete

Facilitation

Focus: Offer a basket of materials to infants and encourage them to place fabric pieces onto the sticky contact paper. Support infants' initiatives and task persistence as they push on and pull off the material.

Comments/Questions: Comment on the colour, texture, type of material the infant chooses.

Describe the infant's actions and consequences.

Look how high you reached!

You made the rice paper stick. Can you pull it off?

Oh, oh, look what happened! You put the red piece on top.

Variation or Extension: Flannel board with sturdy pictures (backed onto cardboard) that are affixed with Velcro, depicting foods, objects, transportation vehicles, and clothing, all from different cultures.

ACTIVITY 14 Finger Paint Pictures

► **Age:** 9–18 months

► **Curriculum Area:** Sensory

► **Curriculum Objectives:** Fine-motor manipulation using index finger independently to poke, rub; tactile exploration

► **Developmental Skills:** Visual discrimination; object permanence; receptive/expressive language by identifying pictures, textures

► **Anti-Bias Skill:** To promote familiarity with diversity

► **Materials:** Laminated pictures depicting children of different races, genders, and abilities who are playing, eating, sleeping; finger-paints of various colours, including skin tones

► **Level:** Concrete and representational

Facilitation

Focus: Smear finger-paint on top of the pictures. Encourage infants to move hands in circular fashion and index fingers through the paint, covering and uncovering the pictures, making lines and patterns.

Comments: Describe infants' actions, as well as texture and sensations; label the pictures as they become visible.

You are poking the paint.

It feels cold.

Look what I see. There's a daddy with glasses, just like Trevor's.

Variation or Extension: Finger-painting on a variety of different surfaces: sandpaper of different grades, bubble paper, tin foil, corrugated cardboard, rice paper, etc. Add a scent such as garlic, mint, coriander, vanilla, cinnamon, etc.

ACTIVITY 15 Tapioca Taste

► **Age:** 6–18 months

► **Curriculum Area:** Sensory

► **Curriculum Objectives:** Tactile exploration; fine-motor manipulation by squeezing, releasing, and dropping; sensory pleasure

► **Developmental Skills:** Eye-hand coordination; receptive language, associating body parts with labels

► **Anti-Bias Skill:** To promote sense of

agency and exposure to new experience

► **Materials:** Water bin, brown water, clear tapioca (which when cooked results in glutinous balls), or coloured tapioca made with nontoxic paint in primary colours, small containers from various cultures to act as scoopers

► **Level:** Concrete

Facilitation

Focus: Encourage infants to grasp, squeeze,

release, scoop up tapioca during water play. Comment on the slippery, bumpy texture, the colour, position in the water, i.e., floating, on the bottom, etc.

Comments: Nicole, you're squeezing the tapioca. It's slippery.

Nashwa is using the ladle.

Look how many you scooped up (or label whatever container is being used).

Oh-oh, Nashwa dropped the blue/red/brown one.

Variation or Extension: Finger-paint with boiled tapioca and paint. Focus on the interesting patterns that emerge.

ACTIVITY 16   Symphony of Pots and Pans

▶ **Age:** 12–18 months

▶ **Curriculum Area:** Motor

▶ **Curriculum Objectives:** Fine-motor—grasping, targeting, and hitting; gross-motor—crawling, walking

▶ **Developmental Skills:** Auditory discrimination; causal relationships; expressive and receptive language

▶ **Anti-Bias Skill:** Sense of agency; exposure to various cultural utensils

▶ **Materials:** Wok, pot, degchi, oriental ladle, wooden spoons of various sizes (handle shortened and sanded down for safety); infant swing or any "A" frame. Tie strong string across legs of swing in order to suspend the wok, degchi, and pot from string.

▶ **Level:** Concrete

Facilitation

Focus: Give each infant one of any of the spoons or ladles. Encourage them to walk/crawl around the swing and hit the hanging pots. Comment on the actions and the outcome of sound productions. Label the utensils as they are being hit.

Comments: You're using the ladle. Good banging!

You hit the wok. Lovely loud noise!

Try banging the degchi. Listen, it makes a ringing sound.

Variation or Extension: For younger infants prop them up on your lap and provide smaller plastic utensils for their efforts at targeting and hitting. Crawling infants can be enticed to move toward the suspended pot and produce any sound or movement possible.

ACTIVITY 17   Lazy Susan Patterns

▶ **Age:** 10–18 months

▶ **Curriculum Area:** Motor

▶ **Curriculum Objectives:** Eye-hand coordination; cause and effect; balance and locomotion skills

▶ **Developmental Skills:** Imitation; cause and effect; receptive and expressive language; visual discrimination; spatial relations

▶ **Anti-Bias Skill:** Exposure to areas of bias through pictures; strengthening sense of agency

▶ **Materials:** Lazy Susan, contact paper, pictures depicting children and adults representative of all the diverse areas pasted to the lazy Susan

▶ **Level:** Concrete and Representational

Facilitation

Focus: Encourage the infant to push the lazy Susan, causing it to turn. Once the novelty has worn off, focus the infant's attention on the pictures. Provide appropriate commentary to support language development.

Comments/Questions: Give a push! Look it's going around and around.

Look how quickly it is turning!

Here's a girl playing with blocks. Oops, she's moved over here.

How did she get there? Let's bring her back. Push.

Variation or Extension: Cut thick cardboard into a circle to fit the size of a child's record player. Place it on the "spindle" of the turntable and place a dab of paint on the cardboard. Encourage the infants to "finger-paint" as the record player revolves.

ACTIVITY 18 Package Wrap

▶ *Age:* 9–18 months

▶ *Curriculum Area:* Motor

▶ *Curriculum Objectives:* To practise neat pincer grasp, use of both hands simultaneously; control repetitive actions that produce different sensations

▶ *Developmental Skills:* To let infants practise object permanence; receptive language describing actions and sounds; to foster a sense of achievement

▶ *Anti-Bias Skill:* To promote a sense of agency and exposure to different cultural patterns

▶ *Materials:* Items wrapped in various safe papers, i.e., foil, crepe, wrapping tissue, rice and waxed paper, as well as papers with distinctive patterns. Avoid newspapers, plastic wrap, or anything containing ink or plastic.

▶ *Level:* Concrete

Facilitation

Focus: Encourage the infant to have fun while finding and covering the boxes. Support the child's individual efforts as she approaches the task of wrapping and unwrapping.

Comments/Questions: Describe the child's actions.

What's under the paper? Look, you ripped the paper.

Oh, here's a ball. Can you cover it up again?

Oh, oh, it's gone.

Where did it go?

Variation or Extension: Provide similar paper and add corrugated cardboard, cellophane, or any other safe, easy-to-tear materials. Encourage the infant to tear, shake, crumple, squeeze the paper. Focus the infant's attention on her own actions and the interesting sound effects or visual changes they produce.

ACTIVITY 19   Peg Releasing

▶ **Age:** 10–15 months

▶ **Curriculum Area:** Motor

▶ **Curriculum Objectives:** To gain practice in aim, targeting, release

▶ **Developmental Skills:** Spatial relations; cause and effect; object permanence; receptive language (labelling emotions on faces); visual exploration of happy, sad, angry faces

▶ **Anti-Bias Skill:** To have feelings and emotions labelled

▶ **Materials:** Plastic milk container with pictures that depict families of different ethnic origin, of various ages and abilities; wooden clothespegs with simple faces depicting happy/sad emotions drawn on heads

▶ **Level:** Concrete, representational

Facilitation

Focus: Encourage the infant to imitate your action as you show her how to drop in the clothespegs. Hold the bottle opening toward the clothespeg if the infant is having difficulty. After the clothespegs have successfully been dropped into the container, show the infant how to turn the container upside down, shake it, and watch the pegs fall out. As the pegs come out, direct the infant's attention to the faces on the clothespegs.

Comments/Questions: In goes the clothespeg; now you put one in the container.

Where did the peg go?

Shake, shake—look at the happy face.

Oh, here is the sad face. Drop the peg back in.

Look, who is on the container? That's Grandpa and his friend, who is sitting in a wheelchair.

Variation or Extension: Use an empty coffee can with a plastic lid. Cut a semicircular smile or frown on the lid and draw in the remaining facial features. Encourage the infant to associate words with his actions; compare happy/sad face on the can and pull off the lid to find the clothespegs. To sustain the exposure to cultural differences, look for coffee tins from other countries. Follow up with songs on emotions, i.e., "If you're happy and you know it ..."

ACTIVITY 20   Lids and Containers

▶ **Age:** 12–18 months

▶ **Curriculum Area:** Motor

▶ **Curriculum Objectives:** Fine-motor coordination in pulling, pushing, screwing, and unscrewing; visual discrimination of shape and size

▶ **Developmental Skills:** Trial-and-error approach to problem-solving; making decisions

▶ **Anti-Bias Skill:** To foster a sense of agency; exploration of similarities and differences

▶ **Materials:** A variety of boxes, plastic bottles, and containers with corresponding lids. Provide boxes that reflect different cultures.

▶ **Level:** Concrete

Facilitation

Focus: Encourage the infant to experiment with

containers and their lids, supporting all actions and choices. Describe how the lids fit/don't fit and the actions required to get them on and off. Eventually the infant will distinguish which lids have to be turned and which have to be placed. To stimulate curiosity, add small, noisy objects inside.

Comments: Let's try to pull this lid off. Good pulling, Jason, you got it off.

Oh-oh, this lid is too big. It won't fit.

You are trying so hard to put the lid on.

Almost … you need this one, it is a square.

Variation or Extension: Commercial shape sorters continue the practice of problem-solving with shapes and spatial dimensions

WORKING IT THROUGH

Design and lay out a one-week anti-bias program plan (use Chart 7.2). Develop five activities across the required developmental domains using either the developmental-based skill approach or the theme-based approach.

Identify the areas of bias and the anti-bias skills for each activity.

Example:

Development-based skill	Theme-based
Drawing relationships	Family
Sense of agency	Friends
Spatial relations	Toys

WEEKLY PLAN					
AGE: INFANT	SKILL ☐ THEME-RELATED ☐ (✓ BOX) IDENTIFY SKILL/THEME:				
	Language	**Socioemotional**	**Sensory**	**Motor**	**Remarks**
Monday					
A-B AREA					
A-B SKILL					
Tuesday					
A-B AREA					
A-B SKILL					
Wednesday					
A-B AREA					
A-B SKILL					
Thursday					
A-B AREA					
A-B SKILL					
Friday					
A-B AREA					
A-B SKILL					
Dramatic/Social Play Props		Water Table Play Props		Sand Table Play Props	

CHART 7.2

Source: Hall and Rhomberg.

Developmental-Based Toddler Activities within an Anti-Bias Framework

PURPOSE

- To enable the practitioner to explore the range of activities appropriate for toddlers within an anti-bias framework

STRATEGIES

- Designed and formatted activities that include anti-bias skills for each developmental domain for ages 18–30 months
- Explanation of the interaction process found in the "facilitation" portion of each activity
- Suggested implementation techniques to convey the anti-bias approach

MAKING THE CONNECTION

- To understand through the presentation of a completed weekly program plan, with anti-bias sections, how children can:
  1) practise anti-bias skills on a daily basis
  2) be exposed to each area of bias at least once a week

Activities for Toddlers

For teachers working with toddlers, the primary task in the affective domain continues to be promoting a positive sense of self. The relationship with family members is an important aspect of toddler identity and needs to be emphasized during interactions and activities. This can be done through exposure to pictures, books, audio tapes, and special family items. As with the infant age group, exposure is still the principle method in introducing anti-bias concepts; however, the emphasis placed on adult-child interaction is significantly different with the toddler age group.

Toddlers need to hear labelled not only their actions but also how feelings are connected. Similarly, toddlers are beginning to discriminate basic differences in size, shape, and colour. Teachers should make an effort to link toddlers' play with clearly identified labels of how things/people/events are similar and different. These simplified conversations are the scaffolding which, with increasing regularity and breadth of content, will strengthen toddlers' self-awareness and build an enriched awareness of others. In this way the rudimentary idea of diversity is communicated to toddlers in a developmentally appropriate manner.

The inclusion of diverse sensory materials encourages toddlers to try new experiences. Such materials can consist of:

- sounds—songs, finger plays, stories in different languages
        —music with various instruments
- smells—spices, herbs, soaps, and extracts
- textures—fabrics, natural and man-made materials
- tastes—food and drink from different cultures
- visual images—posters, photos, books, as well as objects that reflect diversity across the areas of gender, age, ability, race, culture, and appearance.

In this concerted way, teachers reduce the inflexibility and resistance to novelty that can occur at a later stage of development.

The activities in this chapter are all developmentally based.

CHART 8.1

WEEKLY PLAN					
AGE: TODDLER	**SKILL ☑ THEME-RELATED ☐ (✓ BOX) IDENTIFY SKILL/THEME: DRAWING RELATIONSHIPS**				
	Language	**Socioemotional**	**Cognitive/Fine Motor**	**Sensory**	**Gross Motor**
Monday	Flip Book of Actions and Feelings	Notes to Families	Magnet Patterns	Tall Textured Boards	Sorting Shelves
A-B AREA	Gender	All areas	All areas	Culture	Gender-culture
A-B SKILL	Awareness of others' feelings	Self-esteem	Similarities/ differences	Similarities/ differences	Promote gender equity
Tuesday	"Routines" Feely Box	Band-Aids on Dolls	Muffin-Tin Puzzles	Paint and Peel	Hats and Headwear Game
A-B AREA	Gender-culture	Race-gender	Race	Culture	Culture
A-B SKILL	Self-worth	Uniqueness of self and others	Self-concept	Exposure to cultural symbols	Similarities/ differences
Wednesday	Book of Family Gatherings	Life Cycle of the Toddler	Nesting and Stacking Games	Helping with Chores	Bags in a Basket
A-B AREA	Culture	Gender	Culture	Gender-culture	All areas
A-B SKILL	Value uniqueness of each family	Self-esteem	Similarities/ differences	Nonstereotypical	Similarities/ differences
Thursday	Hello, Goodbye Signing	Making Faces	Shoe Sort	Bumpy Paint Braille	Picture Blocks
A-B AREA	Ability	Race	Culture-gender	Ability-race	All areas
A-B SKILL	Ability to interact with diversity	Similarities/ differences	Value self and others	Exposure to new experiences	Foster self-identity
Friday	The Girl Who Needs Glasses	Visiting Guests	Mailing Letters	Cubic Painting	Delivering Mail
A-B AREA	Ability	Age-ability	Culture	Race-culture	Gender
A-B SKILL	Familiarity with differences	Interact with diversity	Self-esteem	Positive sense of self	Promote gender equity
Dramatic/Social Play Props		Water Table Play Props		Sand Table Play Props	

Source: Hall and Rhomberg.

ACTIVITY 1   Flip Book of Actions and Feelings

▶ **Age:** 18–30 months

▶ **Curriculum Area:** Language

▶ **Curriculum Objectives:** To identify emotional states and learn the words to describe them; to help toddler learn to predict cause and effect

▶ **Developmental Skills:** Visual discrimination; building trust and emotional security; fine-motor coordination

▶ **Anti-Bias Skill:** To become aware of others' feelings; to build security of each toddler

▶ **Materials:** Design a book (whose pages are held together with loose-leaf rings) that illustrates a toddler crying, smiling, laughing, angry, frustrated, sad, content on one side, with a matching picture of a toddler being fed, cuddled, given a toy, changed, building blocks on the other side; cardboard, contact paper, pictures depicting children of all races, cultures, abilities; two loose-leaf rings

▶ **Level:** Representational

Facilitation

Focus: Clearly identify how the child in the picture is feeling, linking it to the cause. Encourage the toddler to turn the page to find out how the mother/father/grandparent helped the child cope with his emotions, and point out the solution. Find examples that reflect the toddler's daily emotional situations.

Hearing, seeing, and recognizing feelings will help the toddler gain understanding and control of his or her emotions.

Comments: This baby is sad—her diaper is dirty. Oh, look, Daddy is changing her dirty diapers. That makes her feel good.

This baby is sad—she is hungry. Look, Mommy is giving her a bottle. That makes her feel happy.

This baby is happy—Grandma is rocking her in the chair.

This baby looks scared. She sees a stranger. Look, Mommy is cuddling her and telling her, "I'm here with you."

ACTIVITY 2   "Routines" Feely Box

▶ **Age:** 20–30 months

▶ **Curriculum Area:** Expressive Language

Curriculum Objectives: To identify common objects associated with specific routines; visual memory

▶ **Developmental Skills:** Temporal sequencing; relational thinking; tactile discrimination

▶ **Anti-Bias Skill:** To foster positive self-concept; to value the uniqueness of self and others

▶ **Materials:** Large covered box with opening filled with a toothbrush, a washcloth, different types of combs, brushes, sea sponge, bedtime objects, and books such as *Goodnight Moon*, *Wake Up and Goodnight*, *Talk about Bedtime*, etc.

▶ **Level:** Concrete and representational

Facilitation

Focus: Allow each toddler to reach into the box, touch an object, and try to guess what it is before it is pulled out. Encourage children to identify what the object is and help them to tell when and what they use it for. Try to make toddlers aware of the routines they do in the morning and the routines they do at nighttime.

Comments: This is Indra's brush.

Show us how you brush your hair, Indra.

This is Soonoo's comb. It looks different. Soonoo, show us how you comb your hair.

Label items as children pull them out, if children are unable to do so.

Help children to see the commonalities in their routines and what makes the differences special.

Variation or Extension: Read above-mentioned books and sing lullabies that represent the cultural diversity of your group and staff.

ACTIVITY 3 Book of Family Gatherings

▶ **Age:** 18-30 months

▶ **Curriculum Area:** Language

▶ **Curriculum Objectives:** Visual memory; providing opportunity to identify family members and events; strengthening attachment relationship

▶ **Developmental Skills:** Visual discrimination; promotion of positive sense of self and group belonging

▶ **Anti-Bias Skill:** To value the uniqueness of the child's own family and other families; to promote an understanding of the child's relation to his family

▶ **Materials:** Photo albums with peel-back pages, pictures of children in your group with their families (including extended members). Have photos of memorable events such as birthdays, picnics, celebrations, or any special times spent together.

▶ **Level:** Representational

Facilitation

Focus: Use any opportunity to sit and look at individual albums either on a one-to-one basis or in a small group. Identify people in the photo in relationship to the child and describe the nature of the event. Ensure that each child feels affirmed and gains a sense of belonging to the family grouping.

Comments/Questions: Look, here is Madeleine sitting on Grandmother's lap. They are on the grass having a picnic.

Let's see if we can find Jonah's grandmother. Are they having a picnic?

No, they are lighting candles. Jonah is celebrating Chanukah.

ACTIVITY 4 Hello, Goodbye Signing

▶ **Age:** 24–30 months

▶ **Curriculum Area:** Expressive and Receptive Language

▶ **Curriculum Objectives:** To communicate key phrases in different languages (those represented in your group, including signing), eye-hand coordination, and visual discrimination

▶ **Developmental Skills:** Auditory discrimination and memory

▶ **Anti-Bias Skill:** To increase the toddler's ability to interact with others who are different; to promote awareness of the cultures and abilities of others

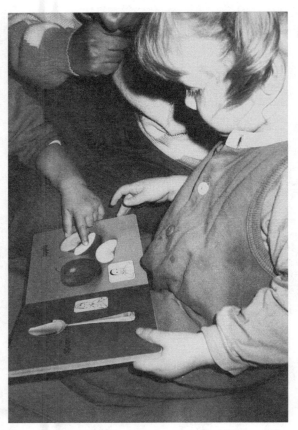

Increasing the toddler's ability to interact with others who are different.

▶ **Materials:** Felt pieces and board to illustrate a story relevant to your group.

▶ **Level:** Representational and Symbolic

Facilitation

Focus: Present a felt-board story about children from different countries who need to learn how to communicate with each other in order to play. Ask the children to help by repeating key phrases such as hello, goodbye, please, thank you, no, yes. Include demonstration of signs. End with songs such as "Aroom Sum Sum" or "Skinnymarink" which involve action gestures.

Note: Keep using different languages and signing throughout the year where appropriate.

Comments/Questions: Maria, let's tell everyone here how your family says goodbye—say Ciao.

Antoine, tell everyone here how your family says hello—Bonjour.

Continue until each child and staff member has been acknowledged.

Make sure you address any child's inappropriate response to the unfamiliar phrase by saying, "This is how Antoine's family says hello. It sounds different to you. We can say hello in different ways."

Variation or Extension: Provide books that are dual track so the children become familiar with stories relayed in two languages

---

ACTIVITY 5 ## The Girl Who Needs Glasses

▶ **Age:** 24–30 months

▶ **Curriculum Area:** Language

▶ **Curriculum Objectives:** To listen and follow a felt-board story; to label body parts

▶ **Developmental Skills:** To promote a positive self-concept

▶ **Anti-Bias Skill:** To learn about differences in abilities

▶ **Materials:** Persona doll with glasses; felt pieces that represent the story

▶ **Level:** Representational

Facilitation

Focus: Develop a simple story about a child who needs glasses (braces, asthma mask, hearing aid, etc.). Introduce the idea through a persona doll who is wearing glasses. Point out anyone in the

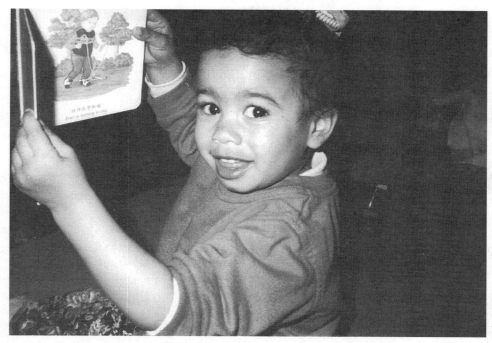

Promoting awareness of other's abilities.

room, child or staff, who is wearing glasses.
Comments/Questions: The story should focus on
healthy body parts and what they are used for,
and how doctors help when the body part

doesn't work well.
Variation or Extension: Create a similar story for a
hearing-impaired, physically challenged, or
asthmatic child.

ACTIVITY 6 Notes to Families

▶ *Age:* 18–30 months

▶ *Curriculum Area:* Socioemotional

▶ *Curriculum Objectives:* An opportunity to work through issues of attachment and
separation; to strengthen the child's sense of
security

▶ *Developmental Skills:* To hear and
learn words for feelings relating to attachment
and separation; fine-motor coordination

▶ *Anti-Bias Skill:* To promote an understanding of the child's relation to own family,
sense of self-esteem

▶ *Materials:* Paper, large crayons,
envelopes, stickers

▶ *Level:* Representational and Symbolic

Facilitation

Focus: Suggest to the toddlers that their
mothers/fathers (grandparents/aunts, etc.) miss
them and would love to get a special letter from
them. Encourage children to practise scribbling
with crayons. As they are drawing, focus the
conversation on the activities that the child has
done, i.e., snack, outdoor play, singing, reading,
etc. Talk about parents at work and offer words

for feelings and ideas. Jot down key words and the child's name on paper. Let the child stuff the note in an envelope and put it in a cubby for safe keeping. Use terms of endearment unique to each family.

Comments: Let's tell Mommy/Bubbie what you played with today.

Mommy really misses you at work. She wants to hug you and kiss you.

Mommy will be so happy/excited to read your letter!

Variation or Extension: Chatting on phones. Encourage toddlers to participate in a conversation with you and their family. Emphasize words for feelings and activities.

ACTIVITY 7   Band-Aids on Dolls

▶ **Age:** 18–30 months

▶ **Curriculum Area:** Socioemotional

▶ **Curriculum Objectives:** To strengthen self-identity, sense of trust, and security; to build empathy

▶ **Developmental Skills:** Eye-hand coordination; pincer grasp; causal relations; expressive language; sense of group belonging

▶ **Anti-Bias Skill:** Valuing uniqueness of self and others; to develop empathy

▶ **Materials:** Dolls of different races and abilities (i.e., brace, different skin tones, hearing aid, etc.), transparent Band-Aids, rolls of gauze, scissors

▶ **Level:** Concrete

Facilitation

Focus: Encourage children to look after dolls that are hurt. Assist them as they experiment with the materials. Comment on how the hurt is being looked after and how the children are making the dolls feel better, just like their families make them feel better. Make casual reference to how you can see the colour of the skin through the Band-Aid/gauze.

Comments/Questions: Dolly hurt her arm.

You're using the Band-Aid to make her feel better.

Good job wrapping (sticking it on)!

We can still see the skin. Does it look like yours?

ACTIVITY 8   Life Cycle of the Toddler

▶ **Age:** 24–30 months

▶ **Curriculum Area:** Socioemotional

▶ **Curriculum Objectives:** To identify objects that babies and toddlers use differently and in the same way; to promote self-esteem

▶ **Developmental Skills:** Visual discrimination; receptive and expressive language

▶ **Anti-Bias Skill:** To foster positive self-esteem

▶ **Materials:** Cover a large surprise box to hold the following props/picture from the families: newborn/toddler diapers, powder, pacifier, bottle/cup, baby toy (rattle), toddler toy hairbrush, infant sleeper/toddler clothes, picture of highchair/table, change table, and potty, picture of crawler/walker

▶ **Level:** Concrete and Representational

Facilitation

Focus: Encourage the toddler to sort what a baby needs, uses, and does in contrast to the toddler. Support all answers while helping them recognize themselves as individuals.

Comments/Questions: Hold up a rattle. Look what I found! Does anybody remember what this is?

Yes, it's a rattle.

Babies love to shake it, make noise with it, and suck it.

Look at this rattle. Does it look the same?

What do we use it for? That's right, Jess, you play music with it.

What about this baby bottle?

ACTIVITY 9 — Making Faces

► **Age:** 18–30 months

► **Curriculum Area:** Socioemotional

► **Curriculum Objectives:** To strengthen self-image through representational pictures; body awareness

► **Developmental Skills:** Eye-hand coordination; relational thinking; visual discrimination

► **Anti-Bias Skill:** To promote awareness of similarities and differences in children's facial features

► **Materials:** Cutouts from magazines of lips, eyes, noses, ears, and hair, sorted in containers; different skin-coloured paper (people paper) cut in circles, glue and paddles.

► **Level:** Representational

Facilitation

Focus: Encourage toddlers to select facial features, identifying each cutout chosen. Relate representational body part to the toddler's own face. Allow the toddler to place cutouts anywhere on the circle. Direct the child to think about what's missing rather than telling the child.

Comments: For older toddlers, point out the differences in eye colour, hair type, glasses, if depicted, and skin colour. The conversation should be natural, not forced. Any negative comments by the children in relation to appearance should be clarified immediately.

ACTIVITY 10 — Visiting Guests

► **Age:** 18–30 months

► **Curriculum Area:** Socioemotional

► **Curriculum Objectives:** To enhance sense of family; self-esteem; social interactions with others' family members

► **Developmental Skills:** Expressive and receptive language; labelling of feelings and relationships

► **Anti-Bias Skill:** Affirmation of self in relation to family; exposure to differences through interactions with diverse people

► **Materials:** Invite adults representing as many areas of diversity as possible to visit classroom. Make sure to include family members in your group (people of different ages, cultures, racial backgrounds, and abilities, with seeing-eye dog, e.g., or someone in a wheelchair).

► **Level:** Concrete

Facilitation

Focus: Have adults engage toddlers in a wide variety of activities, such as painting, reading, gross-motor games, puzzles, and so on. Be sure to avoid "stereotypical" images when encouraging adult interactions, i.e., a person in a wheelchair should be involved in a ball toss as opposed to only sitting "quietly" and reading. Visits should be encouraged frequently.

Comments: That's Kisha's grandmother. She's skipping to the music with you.

Olga's uncle is having fun with the cookie cutters.

ACTIVITY 11 ## Magnet Patterns

▶ **Age:** 24–30 months

▶ **Curriculum Area:** Cognitive/Fine Motor

▶ **Curriculum Objectives:** Visual discrimination of shape and size; eye-hand coordination; reproducing patterns

▶ **Developmental Skills:** Cause and effect, relational thinking; receptive language relating to size, shape, and spatial position

▶ **Anti-Bias Skill:** To promote awareness of similarities and differences

▶ **Materials:** Large clipboard, magnetic strips, glue, assortment of hardware nuts and bolts in varying shapes and sizes (avoid smallest size for safety)

▶ **Level:** Concrete

Facilitation

Focus: Encourage the toddler to experiment with scientific concepts of magnetism. As the novelty wears off, create a simple pattern of alternating big and small nuts (two, then four, etc.) and prompt the toddler to replicate it. Bring out the board the next day and see whether the pattern with different shaped hardware can be reproduced.

Comments/Questions: Language relating to names of shapes (round, circle) and sizes (big, little) should be used. Gradually introduce positional terms such as over, under, next to.

Variation or Extension: Create your own magnets by laminating pictures of adults and children interacting in playing, feeding, sleeping, bathing. Glue magnetic strips onto the backs of these pictures. Encourage toddlers to sort pictures according to category of activity, or create their own pattern.

ACTIVITY 12   Muffin-Tin Puzzles

▶ **Age:** 18–30 months

▶ **Curriculum Area:** Cognitive/Fine Motor

▶ **Curriculum Objectives:** Visual discrimination of size; eye-hand coordination, and matching

▶ **Developmental Skills:** Visual association of emotions; identifying emotions; spatial exploration

▶ **Anti-Bias Skill:** To foster self-concept and an awareness of different races

▶ **Materials:** Muffin tins of varying sizes to accommodate ping pong or tennis balls marked to portray happy or sad faces in skin-tone colours; pictures of happy/sad faces of children from different races glued arbitrarily or in a patterned sequence inside the bottom of the tins

▶ **Level:** Concrete and representational

Facilitation

Focus: To challenge the toddler's matching abilities while simultaneously allowing her to enjoy putting in and taking out balls from puzzle holes. Ask the toddler to identify the faces as happy or sad. Count the happy faces together.
Comments/Questions: Good matching!
   Is it a happy face or a sad face?
   Show me your sad face.
Variation or Extension: Make a more complicated matching puzzle by gluing coloured strips in the tins and providing balls of identical colours.

ACTIVITY 13   Nesting and Stacking Games

▶ **Age:** 18–30 months

▶ **Curriculum Area:** Cognitive

▶ **Curriculum Objectives:** To help classify similar objects by size and shape; problem-solving through trial and error

▶ **Developmental Skills:** Eye-hand coordination; spatial relations; language related to labelling sizes and shapes

▶ **Anti-Bias Skill:** To explore similarities and differences

▶ **Materials:** Variety of culturally diverse nesting objects, i.e., Russian "Matroshki" dolls, Japanese boxes, Chinese bamboo steamers

▶ **Level:** Concrete

Facilitation

Focus: To ensure success, start the toddler with big objects first and only offer three at a time to minimize confusion. Demonstrate putting smaller objects on top of larger, or vice versa. Direct the toddler to imitate, "You put the little box in the big box" or "Look, I'm hiding the little doll under the big doll." Praise correct choices and offer help by suggesting, "try this one," if he makes a mistake.
Comments: The toddler needs plenty of opportunities to explore and experiment to perfect the understanding of size graduation.

ACTIVITY 14 Shoe Sort

▶ *Age:* 18–30 months

▶ *Curriculum Area:* Cognitive

▶ *Curriculum Objectives:* Visual discrimination of a matching set; visual memory of personal items; labelling of the child's own and others' possessions

▶ *Developmental Skills:* Matching according to shape, size, or colour; labelling types of footwear; awareness of others in the group

▶ *Anti-Bias Skill:* To foster a sense of self; to value uniqueness of self and others

▶ *Materials:* Children's running shoes, boots, slippers, adults' sandals, walking shoes, and thongs

▶ *Level:* Concrete

Facilitation

Focus: Bring out a collection of shoes in pairs that reflect not only a variety of footwear but also a cross-representation of children and adults in the toddler group. Assist the children to observe and try to identify which shoes belong to which people. Point out differences in types of footwear and label what kinds of shoes they are playing with. Encourage toddlers to sort shoes and create pairs.

Comments/Questions: Good for you, Marta, you found your running shoes. They look different from Tyler's.

Tyler, your running shoes are black.

Bill, you have one sandal and one slipper. Can you find another shoe that looks like this slipper?

Whose boots are these? They are big. That's right, they belong to your teacher, Indra.

Variation or Extension: For older toddlers (24–30 months), provide two bins decorated to indicate winter and summer. Have footwear properly grouped. As you bring out the footwear, encourage toddlers to identify the type and ask them when they wear them—in the summer or the winter. Let toddlers play with the footwear and create groupings in whatever way they wish.

ACTIVITY 15 Mailing Letters

▶ *Age:* 24–30 months

▶ *Curriculum Area:* Cognitive

▶ *Curriculum Objectives:* To practise folding paper and stuffing envelopes; following a two-step process

▶ *Developmental Skills:* Using both hands together; spatial relations; pride in own accomplishments.

▶ *Anti-Bias Skill:* To promote positive self-esteem

▶ *Materials:* Small squared papers, crayons, envelopes with different scripts, stamps from different countries

▶ *Level:* Concrete

Facilitation

Focus: Reinforce that families miss the children during the day and that a letter from the children is fun for parents/grandparents to read. Let children explore how to fold and unfold paper as well as stuff and unstuff envelopes.

Comments: Encourage toddlers to tell you who the letter is for, and talk about what is important to the child.

Variation or Extension: For children with refined

pincer coordination, provide stickers to pull off and place on the envelopes as stamps.

ACTIVITY 16 Tall Textured Boards

▶ *Age:* 18–30 months

▶ *Curriculum Area:* Sensory

▶ *Curriculum Objectives:* Tactile exploration; visual and tactile discrimination; matching

▶ *Developmental Skills:* Spatial judgment; targeting; fine-motor coordination; receptive language relating to sensations

▶ *Anti-Bias Skill:* To promote exploration of similarities and differences; to work cooperatively

▶ *Materials:* Large felt board, Velcro tabs, identical pairs of texture boards (5 cm squares), which can be affixed to feltboard. Texture boards should be covered with burlap, wool, silk, wood, metal wires (safely secured), rubber, velvet, etc.

▶ *Level:* Concrete

Facilitation

Focus: Encourage toddlers to stick boards up and then find the matched pair. Demonstrate how one board can be placed onto and removed from another. Initially, the attention may focus on ripping the boards off the Velcro; however, gently focus the children's attention to how each square feels and looks.

Comments/Questions: Can you find another square just the *same* as this one?

You found one with wood. Feel how smooth both these squares are.

When an incorrect match occurs, comment "You're right, these two are both purple but they feel different. This one is scratchy and this one is smooth."

During this activity, emphasize things that look and feel the same/different.

Variation or Extension: Texture Lotto. One large texture board full of small squares with matching pieces in a separate container.

ACTIVITY 17 Paint and Peel

▶ *Age:* 18–30 months

▶ *Curriculum Area:* Sensory

▶ *Curriculum Objectives:* Tactile, visual, olfactory exploration; fine-motor manipulation; object permanence

▶ *Developmental Skills:* Cause and effect—on and off; visual discrimination; receptive and expressive language

▶ *Anti-Bias Skill:* Exposure to various cultural symbols

▶ *Materials:* Large cutout characters from a variety of different scripts, i.e., English, First Nations, Greek, Japanese, Urdu, Arabic, Hebrew, etc.; large mirror, finger-paint scented with spices, clear tape

▶ *Level:* Representational

Facilitation

Focus: Place mirror, taped with characters, on low table. Place dabs of paint in strategic places and encourage the toddler to cover the paper cutouts and the mirror; when the toddler begins to pick at the paper, encourage him to peel it off and focus on the shape that has been created. Let the toddler cover it up with the paint and make it disappear. Repeat the activity with all of the stencil cutouts. Do not emphasize the letter aspect, but rather how a shape can appear and disappear.

Comments/Questions: You're using your whole hand to cover that shape.

Round and round; you're smearing the paint

all over the mirror. Look, you've covered up all the shapes.

Where did they go? Do you want to find them again? Let's peel one off.

Pull it off. You did it!

Look, there's the mirror again. Who do you see? It's you, Bobby.

Variation or Extension: Use individual mirrors and whipped Ivory Snow detergent (the only non-allergenic detergent mild enough for children this young).

ACTIVITY 18   Helping with Chores—Washing and Drying Clothes

▶ **Age:** 18–30 months

▶ **Curriculum Area:** Sensory

▶ **Curriculum Objectives:** To provide opportunities for sensory pleasure; fine-motor coordination

▶ **Developmental Skills:** Temporal sequence; causal relations; language relating to labelling actions in the process

▶ **Anti-Bias Skill:** Participation in a non-stereotypical activity

▶ **Materials:** Multiracial dolls, clothing, basin, Ivory Liquid (the only non-allergenic dish liquid mild enough for children this young), clothesline, pegs

▶ **Level:** Concrete

Facilitation

Focus: Capitalize on toddlers' eagerness to imitate chores they see parents doing, along with the opportunity to engage in water play. Talk about why and when clothes need washing and what happens to clothes after they are wet. Support the toddlers' initiatives relating to the actual process of washing and hanging up the clothing. Emphasize gender equity in this activity.

Comments/Questions: During the process of the activity comment on the different ways of washing/drying clothes. Ask or point out how clothes are dried in the day care; point out similarities and differences in the way families carry out this task.

Variation or Extension: Take a walk in the neighbourhood and point out the variety of clotheslines (circular, racks, lines) as well as the machines in a laundromat.

ACTIVITY 19 Bumpy Paint Braille

► *Age:* 18–30 months

► *Curriculum Area:* Sensory

► *Curriculum Objectives:* Tactile and visual exploration

► *Developmental Skills:* Expressive and receptive language; fine-motor manipulation

► *Anti-Bias Skill:* Exposure to the concept of Braille and a variety of skin-tone paints

► *Materials:* Prepare Braille letters on placemat-size construction paper. Use peas or beans to make the dot configuration of letters selected for each mat. Laminate or cover mat with clear contact paper after peas have been glued or taped. Above each Braille configuration, print the letter it represents (use letters of children's first names), various paint colours, including a variety of skin-tone colours.

► *Level:* Representational and Symbolic

Facilitation

Focus: Let toddlers select a placemat. Encourage them to use their fingers and hands as they paint over the peas. Promote awareness of Braille by commenting on letters and configuration.

Comments/Questions: Feel the mat. It's bumpy.
Here's the letter for your name. That's A for Alec.
Feel the letter. It is bumpy.
Lots of dots here.

Variation or Extension: Textured painting. Use various textures in the finger-paint, such as oatmeal, salt, sawdust, or cornmeal to enhance the sensory experience.

ACTIVITY 20 Cubic Painting

► *Age:* 18–30 months

► *Curriculum Area:* Sensory

► *Curriculum Objectives:* To experience tactile sensation of cold temperature; comparison and awareness of skin-colour shades

► *Developmental Skills:* Fine-motor coordination; causal relations as ice cubes melt

► *Anti-Bias Skill:* To foster a positive sense of self and an awareness of different races

► *Materials:* Prepare a variety of ice cubes with people-coloured paint. Supply each child with white paper.

► *Level:* Concrete

Facilitation

Focus: Encourage each child to select several ice cubes and manipulate them on paper (up and down, circular, etc.). Focus their attention on the changes that are taking place: (1) the ice cube melting as a result of warm hands; (2) the paper changing colour as a result of the ice cube melting onto it.

Comments/Questions: Use the opportunity for incidental teaching about skin colour by comparing the ice cubes to the child's own skin or to the skin of others.

Variation or Extension: Add scents to the ice cubes; better still if you are able to find/make people-shaped ice cubes.

ACTIVITY 21 — Sorting Shelves

▶ **Age:** 18–30 months

▶ **Curriculum Area:** Gross motor

▶ **Curriculum Objectives:** To practise stooping, lifting, carrying; visual discrimination and matching like objects

▶ **Developmental Skills:** Making decisions; expressive language

▶ **Anti-Bias Skill:** To promote gender equity in dramatic centre; an awareness of cultural differences in similar tools

▶ **Materials:** Props from dramatic play centre: breads from around the world, baskets, cooking utensils (thava, griddle, wok, bamboo rice spoon, steamers, metal pot, metal steamer, garlic press); dishes, cups, eating utensils; boxes and packages of foods that represent different cultures; placemats, etc.

▶ **Level:** Concrete

Facilitation

Focus: Encourage toddlers to clean up their house by organizing their dramatic play props. Provide bins, baskets for sorting.
Comments/Questions: Help the toddlers group categories by asking, "Can you put all the breads/dishes/cups/cooking pots in the basket?"
Variation or Extension: Describe simply how the props are similar.

Allow the toddlers to arrange the materials and bins on the cupboard shelves.

ACTIVITY 22 — Hats and Headwear Game

▶ **Age:** 18–30 months

▶ **Curriculum Area:** Gross motor

▶ **Curriculum Objectives:** Body awareness and coordination; balance

▶ **Developmental Skills:** Eye-hand coordination; object permanence; expressive language; labelling body parts and types of hats

▶ **Anti-Bias Skill:** To strengthen self-concept; exposure to similarities and differences of headgear

▶ **Materials:** Assortment of head wear including: beret, sombrero, yarmulke and other skull caps, mushla, transparent scarves, firefighter hat, police officer's hat, chef's hat, brimmed hats, fur hat, kerchiefs. Make sure that various textures, sizes, and shapes are represented.

▶ **Level:** Concrete

Facilitation

Focus: Encourage toddlers to pull hats/head wear out of a big box, trying them on, walking around with them on, and looking into a mirror. Comment on the characteristics of the head wear and identify it accurately, e.g., "That's a soft, furry, red beret." Expand the game to other body parts besides the head to offer an incongruent experience. Use humour, exaggeration, and enjoy being silly.
Comments/Questions: Place the beret on your toe.
   Where's your toe?
   Does the beret go on your toe? Nooo. It goes on your head.
   Or, where does it go?
Variation or Extension: Use mitts/gloves instead of hats.

ACTIVITY 23 Bags in a Basket

▶ **Age:** 24–30 months

▶ **Curriculum Area:** Gross motor

▶ **Curriculum Objectives:** To practise carrying, stooping, dumping, and filling large baskets; balance and large-muscle coordination; matching bags by pattern

▶ **Developmental Skills:** Following directions; turn taking

▶ **Anti-Bias Skill:** To promote awareness of similarities and differences

▶ **Materials:** Prepare four groups of two beanbags, each with distinctive cultural patterns. Buy four plastic unicoloured baskets with vertical slots. Weave strips of matching fabric prominently onto one side of each basket.

▶ **Level:** Concrete

Facilitation

Focus: Set up baskets at one end of the playground and hold beanbags in a large container at the other end. Let the toddlers reach in, select a beanbag, look at the pattern, and walk over to the matching basket to drop it in. Explain the game initially by having all the materials together for a demonstration. When the basket is full, the toddler can carry it back and dump the bags in the container. Be flexible around toddler initiatives and own rules.

Comments/Questions: Can you find the basket that looks the same as the beanbag? You found one with zigzag lines.

This one is different. Look at all the colours on this one.

Variation or Extension: Use the same principle but substitute balls of different colours with matching coloured baskets.

ACTIVITY 24 Picture Blocks

▶ **Age:** 18–30 months

▶ **Curriculum Area:** Gross motor

▶ **Curriculum Objectives:** To promote a sense of balance; to explore vertical and horizontal spatial relations

▶ **Developmental Skills:** Visual discrimination; trial and error; eye-hand coordination; matching; receptive language

▶ **Anti-Bias Skill:** To foster strong sense of self-identity; exposure to differences in appearance

▶ **Materials:** Sturdy cardboard boxes made into blocks. Cover with strong paper (use some skin-tone colours), glue no more than two pictures depicting all areas of diversity on each block. Cover each block with clear contact paper.

▶ **Level:** Concrete and representational

Facilitation

Focus: Encourage toddlers to build, carry, and lift blocks; focus their attention on pictures that are the same (that can be matched) and those that are different.

Comments/Questions: Oh, you've found another girl with glasses.

Let's find the man with the beard.

Here's Lida's family. Can you find the same picture on this block?

Good stacking! I like the way you lined up the blocks on the floor.

Using blocks to foster self-identity.

ACTIVITY 25 Delivering Mail

▶ **Age:** 24–30 months

▶ **Curriculum Area:** Gross motor

▶ **Curriculum Objectives:** Large-motor coordination required to carry pouches, pull wagons; sequence of filling, delivering, and distributing mail

▶ **Developmental Skills:** Expressive language in imaginary role-playing

▶ **Anti-Bias Skill:** Gender equity in mail delivery; to promote positive self-esteem

▶ **Materials:** Big pouches/sacks, hats, wagons, homemade mailbox with small cubbies, envelopes

▶ **Level:** Concrete

Facilitation

Focus: Extend the mailing letters activity completed earlier through imaginary role-playing. Help the toddler understand the sequence required by taking an active role as she delivers the mail to you. Toddlers who have a long attention span can insert envelopes into the mailbox and then refill bags.

Comments/Questions: Engage the toddlers in dialogue as they walk around the playground pulling the bags.

"Do you have mail for me today? How lovely, a letter from my friend D——— (a child's name). Will you take this letter and mail it for me? Thank you."

WORKING IT THROUGH

Design and lay out a one-week anti-bias program plan (use Chart 8.2). Develop five activities across the required developmental domains using either the developmental-based skill approach or the theme-based approach.

Identify the areas of bias and the anti-bias skills for each activity.

Example:

Developmental-based skill	Theme-based
Attachment/separation	Family
Imitation	Sounds
Cause and effect	Textures

WEEKLY PLAN					
AGE: INFANT	SKILL ☐ THEME-RELATED ☐ (✓ BOX) IDENTIFY SKILL/THEME:				
	Language	**Socioemotional**	**Cognitive/Fine Motor**	**Sensory**	**Gross Motor**
Monday					
A-B AREA					
A-B SKILL					
Tuesday					
A-B AREA					
A-B SKILL					
Wednesday					
A-B AREA					
A-B SKILL					
Thursday					
A-B AREA					
A-B SKILL					
Friday					
A-B AREA					
A-B SKILL					
Dramatic/Social Play Props		Water Table Play Props		Sand Table Play Props	

CHART 8-2

Source: Hall and Rhomberg.

CHAPTER 9

Theme-Based Preschool-Age Activities within an Anti-Bias Framework

PURPOSE

• To enable the practitioner to explore the range of activities appropriate for preschool-age children within an anti-bias framework

STRATEGIES

• Designed and formatted activities that include anti-bias skills for each developmental domain relevant for the 2-1/2–5-year-old
• Explanation of the interaction process found in the "facilitation" portion of each activity
• Suggested implementation techniques to convey the anti-bias approach

MAKING THE CONNECTION

• To understand through the presentation of a completed weekly program plan, with anti-bias sections, how children can:
1) practise anti-bias skills on a daily basis
2) be exposed to each area of bias at least once a week

Activities for Preschoolers

The role of the teacher with preschool children is to continue exposing and familiarizing them with diversity and promoting a comfort level with such. Assisting children to empathize and problem-solve, however, should be an additional focus as the continuum of developmental skills progresses through to the preschool level. These affective and cognitive skills can be fostered through the routine use of **divergent** and open-ended questions. For example, during storytime, don't be afraid to pause and ask children, "How do you think R felt when others made fun of his ears? What do you think we could do to help R feel better or solve the problem?"

The emerging abilities to identify causal relations and describe solutions to problems speak to the developmental needs of this age group. The adult working with preschool children should be aware that 3–5-year-olds require simultaneous nurturing of those affective and cognitive skills that are linked to anti-bias goals. In this way a dual focus is addressed:

1) Helping children to identify and understand a victim's feelings

2) Encouraging children to think about how to respond to discrimination in a way that supports self-esteem

Although developmental-based activities are the most appropriate approach for all age groups, the predominate method of planning for preschoolers still seems to be thematically based. In view of this trend, this activity section has shifted its focus to the theme Patterns and Rhythms. This idea was previously explored in Chapter 4 from the two curriculum-design perspectives of development and theme.

AGE: PRESCHOOL	SKILL ☐ THEME-RELATED ☑ (✓ BOX)			IDENTIFY SKILL/THEME: PATTERNS & RHYTHMS	
	Language	**Socioemotional**	**Cognitive/ Math, Science**	**Perceptual Motor**	**Gross Motor**
Monday	Pro-Active Cube	Pregnant Mother	Natural Dyes	Thumbs Up and Thumbs Down	Toe Puppets
A-B AREA	All areas	Gender/sexuality	Culture/ability	Ability	Ability
A-B SKILL	Activism, empathetic listening	Exploring alternatives	Try new experiences	Value uniqueness of each child	Promote empathy
Tuesday	Sequence Life Cycle	Ways of Carrying Babies	Tasting Milk	Braille Name Placemats	Bowling
A-B AREA	Age	Culture/ability	Culture	Ability	Ability/culture
A-B SKILL	Challenge stereotypes	Value uniqueness of each family	Exposure to different experiences	Respect different abilities	Similarities/ differences
Wednesday	Hair Alphabet	Feeling Sticks	Matching Spices	Beading	Dances That Tell Stories
A-B AREA	Gender/age/culture	Culture	Culture	Culture	Culture/gender
A-B SKILL	Interact with diversity	Value individual feelings	Awareness of other cultures	Value individuality	Nonstereotypical activities
Thursday	Oral Storytelling Dramatization	Sharing Box	Tangrams	Flag Game	Walking with Different Devices
A-B AREA	Culture	Culture	All areas	Ability/culture	Ability
A-B SKILL	Respect for other cultures	Value contribution of each child	Exposure to diversity	Value diversity	Promote empathy
Friday	Intergenerational Visit	Where Grandparents Came From	Comparing Fresh and Dried Fruits	People Lacing Cards	Basket Balancing
A-B AREA	Age	Culture/age	Age	All areas	Culture/ability/gender
A-B SKILL	Promote respect for seniors	Awareness of stereotypes	Exploring similarities/differences	Awareness of diversity	Awareness of differences/self-esteem
Dramatic/Social Play Props		Water Table Play Props		Sand Table Play Props	

WEEKLY PLAN

CHART 9.1

Source: Hall and Rhomberg.

ACTIVITY 1 Pro-Active Cube

▶ **Age:** 4–5 years

▶ **Curriculum Area:** Language

▶ **Curriculum Objectives:** To practise divergent thinking expressively; listening to others

▶ **Developmental Skills:** Cause and effect; turn taking; problem-solving

▶ **Anti-Bias Skill:** To encourage open-mindedness and promote activism through careful listening

▶ **Materials:** A box (cube) with a picture affixed to each side depicting a situation that children can describe/discuss (box, contact paper, pictures reflecting age, gender, race, ability, appearance; and glue)

▶ **Level:** Representational

Facilitation

Focus: How to voice our opinions; how to identify positive and negative situations/interactions; how to act against social ills such as violence, discrimination, unfairness; how to give and seek help

Comments/Questions: What is happening in the picture?

How does that person's face look? How do you think they feel?

What would you do if you were in this picture/situation?

What would you want another person to do for you?

Variation or Extension: Persona-doll stories that depict incidents of discrimination. (See Derman-Sparks, 1989, for examples.)

ACTIVITY 2 Sequence Life Cycle

▶ **Age:** 3–5 years

▶ **Curriculum Area:** Language

▶ **Curriculum Objectives:** To seriate pictures in order from young to old and to express the relationship

▶ **Developmental Skills:** Scanning pictures; discriminating pictures; temporal ordering

▶ **Anti-Bias Skill:** To foster awareness and challenge stereotypes about senior citizens

▶ **Materials:** Picture cards which depict the cycle of aging (infant, toddler, young child, adolescent, young adult, mid-life, old age). Pictures should portray activities and experiences that are both nonstereotypical and stereotypical in order to promote discussion

▶ **Level:** Representational

Facilitation

Focus: Assist the children to understand the physical changes over time and the process of aging/growing.

Comments/Questions: Who do you see (in each picture)?

What is happening to the person?

What is the person doing?

What is similar about the infant and elderly person?

What is different?

Dispel any misconceived notions based on abilities related to age. Ensure that ageism that discriminates against young or old is included in the discussion. Example:

Child: Look, that old lady is skiing. Grandmas don't ski.

Response: Clarify that just because someone is older doesn't mean that they can't ski. Ask children to talk about all the things that their grandparents/uncles/aunts do and dispel any stereotypes that arise.

Variation or Extension: Life cycle of tree or animal (to compare); visit senior-citizens home; read "The Giving Tree."

ACTIVITY 3 Hair Alphabet

▶ *Age:* 4–5 years

▶ *Curriculum Area:* Language

▶ *Curriculum Objectives:* To identify and label different hair types, styles, and head wear; observation and visual memory

▶ *Developmental Skills:* Scanning pictures; visual discrimination

▶ *Anti-Bias Skill:* To increase children's ability to interact with people different from them

▶ *Materials:* Pictures of hair styles labelled with words (i.e., A is for Afro, B is for Braid, C is for Cowlick; see Appendix, page 149)

▶ *Level:* Representational, Symbolic

Facilitation

Focus: Helping children to see that people (irrespective of gender or age) wear their hair and headgear differently; to encourage children to be open and nonjudgmental when encountering such differences.

Comments/Questions: What kind of hair do you have (colour, texture, style)?

What about your friend—is it the same as yours?

How is it different?

What do you wear on your head or in your hair?

Variation or Extension: Select key styles and head wear and learn how to sign them. Teach these words to the children.

ACTIVITY 4 Oral Storytelling Dramatization

▶ *Age:* 4–5 years

▶ *Curriculum Area:* Language

▶ *Curriculum Objectives:* To become familiar with the tradition of transmitting culture orally (elder to children); listening skills; expressive language

▶ *Developmental Skills:* Memory; problem-solving

▶ *Anti-Bias Skill:* To promote awareness of how culture is passed from generation to generation; respect for other cultures

▶ *Materials:* Guest speaker (storyteller)

▶ *Level:* Concrete and Symbolic

Facilitation

Focus: Discuss style of storytelling (oral). Who tells the story (elder, family members)? What is the content of the stories (nature and morals)? When are they told (daytime, nighttime, at play, etc.)?

Comments/Questions: What kinds of stories are there?

When do you hear stories?

Who tells them?

Which stories do you like?

Variation or Extension: Invite a grandparent to tell a story for circle. Visit a native cultural centre and arrange for a storytelling.

ACTIVITY 5 Intergenerational Visit—
The Story "The Giving Tree"

► **Age:** 3–5 years

► **Curriculum Area:** Language

► **Curriculum Objectives:** Receptive language; temporal ordering; making predictions

► **Developmental Skills:** To promote empathy

► **Anti-Bias Skill:** To promote respect for seniors; to encourage constructing relationships and drawing conclusions

► **Materials:** Visitor; "The Giving Tree"

► **Level:** Symbolic

Facilitation

Focus: Discuss the process of aging and attitude toward seniors.

Comments/Questions: Who/what are our grandparents?

How many grandparents do you have?

What are some special things you do with your grandparents?

Who is old in your family?

What do older people do for us?

Variation or Extension: Regularly scheduled visits by seniors to the centre.

ACTIVITY 6 Pregnant Mother

► **Age:** 4–5 years

► **Curriculum Area:** Socioemotional

► **Curriculum Objectives:** To discuss where babies come from and what mothers do

► **Developmental Skills:** Problem-solving; sequencing; turn taking

► **Anti-Bias Skill:** Explore similarities and differences within families; exposure to alternative lifestyles

► **Materials:** Pregnant mother as visitor

► **Level:** Concrete

Facilitation

Focus: Visitor prompts questions and exploration of motherhood and what it entails. Support the children who may have same-sex families.

Comments/Questions: Who can be a mother?

What does your mom do (as a job or for the child)?

Where do you think babies come from?

Who in your family takes care of you?

Variation or Extension: A mother with a new baby returns for a followup discussion. Read stories that deal with gay families, ie., "Heather has Two Mommies" or "Asha's Mums."

ACTIVITY 7 Ways of Carrying Babies

▶ *Age:* 3–5 years

▶ *Curriculum Area:* Socioemotional

▶ *Curriculum Objectives:* To become familiar with the variety of ways of carrying infants; to support the development of nurturance; self-identity

▶ *Developmental Skills:* Balance and coordination in carrying; eye-hand coordination in tying, wrapping; expressive language

▶ *Anti-Bias Skill:* To respect that babies are carried in different ways in different families; to value the uniqueness of the child's own family and others

▶ *Materials:* Snuggly, cradle board, basket, cloth wrap, car seat, Japanese square, stroller

▶ *Level:* Concrete

Facilitation

Focus: Let the children explore how families have different child-rearing practices; how infants can be carried comfortably in many ways, and the function of a baby carrier.

Comments/Questions: How can we carry a baby?

What are some things we use to carry babies?

How did your parents carry you when you were a baby?

If you had one arm, how would you carry a baby?

Variation or Extension: Provide a variety of carriers in the dramatic play area.

ACTIVITY 8 Feeling Sticks

▶ *Age:* 3–5 years

▶ *Curriculum Area:* Socioemotional

▶ *Curriculum Objectives:* To provide an outlet for the expression of a wide range of emotions; recognition of emotions

▶ *Developmental Skills:* Eye-hand coordination; development of rhythm and pattern recognition

▶ *Anti-Bias Skill:* To value individual feelings; to become aware of individual ways of expressing feelings

▶ *Materials:* Pairs of rhythm sticks

▶ *Level:* Concrete

Facilitation

Focus: This activity helps children understand what emotions are, and how we express feelings. The relationship between feelings and physical responses differ from family to family (and from culture to culture). Make children aware that people respond in different ways to feelings, i.e., not everyone will cry when angry or sad.

Comments/Questions: How do you feel when ...?

What do you do?

If you feel sad, how would you bang the sticks?

This is how I would bang the sticks (demonstrate a different pattern).

Variation or Extension: Look at pictures and discuss their emotional content.

ACTIVITY 9 Sharing Box

▶ **Age:** 3–5 years

▶ **Curriculum Area:** Socioemotional

▶ **Curriculum Objectives:** To strengthen self-identity and pride in family

▶ **Developmental Skills:** Expressive and receptive language; turn taking; sharing; making predictions and comparisons

▶ **Anti-Bias Skill:** To value the contribution of each child

▶ **Materials:** Box and objects from home

▶ **Level:** Concrete

Facilitation

Focus: To bring in objects we use at home (common or uncommon) and share them with the group; how they work, their use, where they come from, etc.

Comments/Questions: Tell me about this object. How do you use it?
  Can I try?
  Can you think of another way to use it?
  Does anyone else have something like this at home?
  What does your family use for sewing? cooking?

Variation or Extension: Ask children who speak a language other than English to teach the name of the object in their language.

ACTIVITY 10 Where Grandparents Came From

▶ **Age:** 3–5 years

▶ **Curriculum Area:** Socioemotional

▶ **Curriculum Objectives:** To strengthen self-concept; promoting value of family members

▶ **Developmental Skills:** Expressive language; problem-solving; listening to others

▶ **Anti-Bias Skill:** To foster awareness of stereotypes associated with the aged; exposure to similarities and differences in families

▶ **Materials:** Map, globe

▶ **Level:** Representational

Facilitation

Focus: To become familiar with individual family roots around the world. To identify similarities and differences among families in the group.

Comments/Questions: What is a grandmother/grandfather?
  Where do your grandparents live?
  What country(ies) did they come from?
  Let's look for that country on the map.
  What kinds of things do you think grandparents do?
  Do you think all grandparents come from the same place?

Variation or Extension: Invite grandparents to visit.

ACTIVITY 11 Natural Dyes

► **Age:** 3–5 years

► **Curriculum Area:** Cognitive

► **Curriculum Objectives:** Cause and effect; change of state; making predictions

► **Developmental Skills:** Fine-motor manipulation; making comparisons; expressive language

► **Anti-Bias Skill:** To promote familiarity with dye making that occurs in different cultures; to try a new experience

► **Materials:** A variety of berries (blueberries, raspberries, cranberries, gooseberries), dandelion flowers, onion, parsley that is either ground or boiled; variety of cloth material

► **Level:** Concrete

Facilitation

Focus: Let the children explore what dyes are made from, how we make them, and what dyes are used for.
Comments/Questions: What are some things we do with berries?
    What kinds of berries can you name?
    What colours are they?
    What colour do you think the dye will be?
    What can we decorate with the dyes?
    Who can make dyes?
    Could I make dyes if I had one arm?
Variation or Extension: Visit a textile store and buy swatches of material to take back to the class. Match dyes, if possible, with the store-bought cloth.

ACTIVITY 12 Tasting Milk

► **Age:** 3–5 years

► **Curriculum Area:** Cognitive

► **Curriculum Objectives:** Taste discrimination; making comparisons and predictions; classifying and grouping

► **Developmental Skills:** Visual and olfactory discrimination; eye-hand coordination in pouring; expressive language in describing and commenting

► **Anti-Bias Skill:** To develop familiarity with a variety of milk types enjoyed by different people

► **Materials:** Milks—homogenized, goat, buttermilk, coconut, soya, baby formula; cups

► **Level:** Concrete

Facilitation

Focus: To taste and compare many kinds of milk
Comments/Questions: Use focus questions.
    What is milk?
    Where does it come from?
    What does it taste like?
    How many kinds are there?
    How is it used?
    How does this milk taste to you?
    Do some taste the same?
    How is the buttermilk different from the plain milk?
Variation or Extension: Visit farm and help milk a cow or goat; make soya milk.

ACTIVITY 13   Matching Spices

▶ **Age:** 3–5 years

▶ **Curriculum Area:** Cognitive

▶ **Curriculum Objectives:** To use our senses of vision and smell to match ground/grated spice to its whole source (i.e., powdered ginger to ginger root); olfactory discrimination

▶ **Developmental Skills:** One-to-one correspondence; making comparisons; part/whole relations

▶ **Anti-Bias Skill:** To promote awareness of other cultures; to try new experiences

▶ **Materials:** Small jars (with perforated lids for smelling), spices, plants, and fruits in their whole and powdered forms, i.e., cinnamon, nutmeg, cloves, garlic, coconut, coffee, peanuts (make certain that no child has a peanut allergy), ginger

▶ **Level:** Concrete

Facilitation

Focus: To provide an opportunity for children to learn what people use to enhance their cooking; how different families might use different ingredients.

Comments/Questions: How does it smell? (sweet? hot?)

Which ones does your family cook with?
What do you make?
Which do you like? Dislike? Why?

Variation or Extension: Cook a simple curry or spice cake. Go to a bulk store and buy spices to cook with.

ACTIVITY 14   Tangrams

▶ **Age:** 3–5 years

▶ **Curriculum Area:** Cognitive

▶ **Curriculum Objectives:** To experiment with shapes/designs using a different type of puzzle; problem-solving; spatial arrangement

▶ **Developmental Skills:** Eye-hand coordination; ordering; one-to-one correspondence if a pattern is used

▶ **Anti-Bias Skill:** To try a new experience; exposure to areas of diversity

▶ **Materials:** Homemade tangram puzzle with pictures representing people of different ages, races, abilities, gender, mounted on cardboard, laminated, and cut

▶ **Level:** Concrete, Representational

Facilitation

Focus: Have the children investigate where the puzzle originates, who plays with it (encourage both girls and boys to experiment with it).

Comments/Questions: How can we arrange the puzzle pieces to make any shape?

What can you see in this pattern?
What do you see on this piece?

Variation or Extension: Read *Grandfather Tang's Story* and have children try to make animal shapes in the story.

ACTIVITY 15   Comparing Fresh and Dried Fruits

▶ **Age:** 3–5 years

▶ **Curriculum Area:** Cognitive

▶ **Curriculum Objectives:** Making observations; temporal ordering; sorting; comparing and classifying

▶ **Developmental Skills:** Expressive language; tactile discrimination

▶ **Anti-Bias Skill:** To increase children's understanding of the aging process; ability to explore similarities and differences

▶ **Materials:** Dried and fresh fruits (i.e., apples, apricots, grapes, raisins, dates, figs)

▶ **Level:** Concrete

Facilitation

Focus: To observe differences between fresh and dried fruits and relate the observations to the process of aging

Comments/Questions: Which fruits are fresh?
   Dry?
   Which fruits can be dried?
   How did that happen?
   This fruit is wrinkled. Do you know people with wrinkled skin?
   Who are they?
   How are they like you?
   How are they different?

Variation or Extension: A fruit-picking excursion.

ACTIVITY 16   Thumbs Up and Thumbs Down

▶ **Age:** 3–5 years

▶ **Curriculum Area:** Perceptual motor

▶ **Curriculum Objectives:** Interpretation of body language; memory; expressive and gestural communication

▶ **Developmental Skills:** Observation; imitation; eye-hand coordination

▶ **Anti-Bias Skill:** To value the uniqueness of each child; to provide the ability to interact with diversity

▶ **Materials:** Pictures of things, events, and situations

▶ **Level:** Representational and Symbolic

Facilitation

Focus: To provide an opportunity to express likes and dislikes.

Comments/Questions: How do you know if you like or dislike something?
   How do you show people that you like or don't like something?
   What is something you like?
   Something you don't like?

Variation or Extension: A tasting game or a favourite-colour game in order to chart likes/dislikes. Children can then visually perceive how they are different and similar and learn to accept that differences are good.

ACTIVITY 17 Braille Name Placemats

▶ **Age:** 4-5 years

▶ **Curriculum Area:** Perceptual motor

▶ **Curriculum Objectives:** Eye-hand coordination; comparison of number and pattern through tactile discrimination

▶ **Developmental Skills:** Counting; cause and effect; letter recognition

▶ **Anti-Bias Skill:** To develop a respect for people with different abilities; to learn to interact with diversity

▶ **Materials:** Stiff paper, pen (to write name on front of card and draw dots on back), thumbtacks (for punching out dots)

▶ **Level:** Concrete and Symbolic

Facilitation

Focus: Let the children explore how people who are blind read, how Braille cards are made, how to write their names in Braille.

Comments/Questions: If you couldn't see, how could you read a book?

How can we use our fingers to read?

What do the bumps mean? Which one is the letter _____?

Show me a letter with the same number of dots.

Variation or Extension: Look and touch real Braille books; feely box games.

ACTIVITY 18 Beading

▶ **Age:** 3–5 years

▶ **Curriculum Area:** Perceptual motor

▶ **Curriculum Objectives:** Eye-hand coordination; sequencing; measurement

▶ **Developmental Skills:** Observation; cause and effect; temporal process; cooperation and turn taking

▶ **Anti-Bias Skill:** Valuing individual creativity; to try an art technique practised widely in many cultures

▶ **Materials:** Dough recipe, natural dyes previously made, skewers, leather laces

▶ **Level:** Concrete

Facilitation

Focus: Children investigate the process involved in making beads. When can colour be added? What ingredients are needed?

Comments/Questions: What shapes can you make other than circles for your beads?

What other materials could you use to make beads?

Ensure that each child's approach to the project is supported.

Variation or Extension: Bring in a wide variety of beads. Make jewellery with corn, seeds, natural clay.

ACTIVITY 19   Flag Game

▶ **Age:** 4–5 years

▶ **Curriculum Area:** Perceptual motor

▶ **Curriculum Objectives:** Visual discrimination; matching patterns, colours, and numbers; eye-hand coordination

▶ **Developmental Skills:** One-to-one correspondence; counting up to 25; classification by colour, pattern, and symbols

▶ **Anti-Bias Skill:** To learn about cultural identity of self, one's family, and others

▶ **Materials:** 1 cm thick sheet of plywood 25 cm x 45 cm mounted on two pieces of wood 6 cm x 15 cm, which serve as stands to lift the board off the table. Lines are drawn about 4 cm from the edges across the board. Slits are drilled every 5 cm along the lines, wide enough to accommodate the width of the popsicle sticks. Miniature pictures of flags are placed in front of the slits. Miniature model flags are made from popsicle sticks and a picture of corresponding flags. Numbers are placed on the back of each flag model which correspond to the flag numbers on the board. This is added to assist children who might find it difficult to match the patterns on the flags. The names of the countries represented by the flags are written in bold letters on the popsicle sticks and on the board.

▶ **Level:** Representational and Symbolic

Facilitation

Focus: Scramble half of the flag models and place them in front of the flags on the board. Allow the children to explore as they wish and observe how they sort and match the flag models to the picture. For those who can manage the challenge, encourage them to mix all 25 flag models.

Comments/Questions: Do you recognize a flag?
    What symbol does Canada have on its flag? What about Turkey?
    Do you know what that symbol is? Krysztof, your mommy and daddy are from Poland. Can you find their flag?
    It is number 7 on the board.
    Jillian was born in Trinidad. Let's try to find the flag of her country.

Variation or Extension: A separate classification game can be encouraged with the use of the flags. Encourage children to classify according to colour, patterns, and symbols in any way they wish.

Source: Ayesha Mondal, Mothercraft student, 1994.

Learning to value one's roots and each others' heritage.

ACTIVITY 20   People Lacing Cards

▶ *Age:* 3–5 years

▶ *Curriculum Area:* Perceptual motor

▶ *Curriculum Objectives:* Eye-hand coordination; sequencing

▶ *Developmental Skills:* Sorting and classifying; expressive language

▶ *Anti-Bias Skill:* To foster awareness of diversity; to strengthen self-identity

▶ *Materials:* Pictures of children and adults (different ages, races, gender, and abilities represented), bristol board, contact paper, yarn, hole puncher

▶ *Level:* Representational

Facilitation

Focus: To manipulate yarn through holes in lacing cards representing different age groups.
Comments/Questions: Which picture is of a baby? an old person?
   How are they alike?
   How are they different?
Variation or Extension: People cards to sequence from infancy to old age.

ACTIVITY 21 Toe Puppets

▶ *Age:* 4–5 years

▶ *Curriculum Area:* Gross motor

▶ *Curriculum Objectives:* To work puppets using body parts other than hands; creative expression

▶ *Developmental Skills:* Eye-foot coordination; expressive language

▶ *Anti-Bias Skill:* To increase children's ability to interact with people different from them; to promote empathy

▶ *Materials:* Toilet rolls and art materials to decorate puppets

▶ *Level:* Concrete

Facilitation

Focus: Explore and compare the different types of puppets that exist and how they are used.
Comments/Questions: Who can use toe puppets?
What kinds of puppets could you use if you had no arms?
How can you make your puppet move sideways? up and down?
How does it feel?
Variation or Extension: Put on a toe-puppet show in a shoe box. Put out many kinds of puppets to compare. Visit a puppet museum.

ACTIVITY 22 Bowling

▶ *Age:* 3–5 years

▶ *Curriculum Area:* Gross motor

▶ *Curriculum Objectives:* Balance; projectile management; eye-hand coordination

▶ *Developmental Skills:* Counting; spatial relations; making predictions; working cooperatively

▶ *Anti-Bias Skill:* To explore differences and similarities (milk containers and coconuts)

▶ *Materials:* Coconut, variety of milk cartons as bowling pins

▶ *Level:* Concrete

Facilitation

Focus: Introduce the skill of bowling, the origins of bowling, and equipment needed.
Comments/Questions: How can we roll the coconut so it knocks down the cartons?
Which rolls faster, the empty one or the one full of milk?
Variation or Extension: Excursion to purchase a coconut.

ACTIVITY 23 Dances That Tell Stories

▶ **Age:** 3–5 years

▶ **Curriculum Area:** Gross motor

▶ **Curriculum Objectives:** Temporal and body awareness; moving body through space; rhythm

▶ **Developmental Skills:** Interpreting; expressive language and imagination

▶ **Anti-Bias Skill:** To experience music and dance from different cultures; nonstereotypical activity for both genders

▶ **Materials:** Knowledge of dance steps, music appropriate for the dance, any necessary props, i.e., scarves, hats, sticks

▶ **Level:** Representational

Facilitation

Focus: To enable the children to explore a different medium of telling stories; to give the children the opportunity to use dance as an expression of ideas.

Comments/Questions: Example: Bird Dance
What are the arms and head telling us?
How do you know?
How would you dance to this music?
What do you think the drum is saying?
What are the bells telling us?

Variation or Extension: Have a dancer from a native cultural centre visit and demonstrate several dances.

ACTIVITY 24 Walking with Different Devices

▶ **Age:** 3–5 years

▶ **Curriculum Area:** Gross motor

▶ **Curriculum Objectives:** Balance and coordination; to improve body and spatial awareness

▶ **Developmental Skills:** Observation; imitation; pride in accomplishment

▶ **Anti-Bias Skill:** To increase children's ability to interact with others who are different from them; to promote empathy

▶ **Materials:** Crutches, snowshoes, flippers, can stilts, cane, etc.

▶ **Level:** Concrete

Facilitation

Focus: To encourage children to try walking with different devices. Focus their attention on how it feels. Identify and clarify any stereotypes that may surface.

Comments/Questions: How do we walk?
What are things that help us walk?
How does it feel, and why? What is this (cane)?
Why or when would someone use it?
Who do you know that uses it?
How does this device work?

Variation or Extension: Try three-legged races; make can stilts; make flipper footprints with paint.

ACTIVITY 25   Basket Balancing

▶ *Age:* 4–5 years

▶ *Curriculum Area:* Gross motor

▶ *Curriculum Objectives:* Balance; coordination; spatial and body awareness

▶ *Developmental Skills:* Imitation; pride in achievement

▶ *Anti-Bias Skill:* To promote awareness of cultural traditions; to foster self-esteem; to try a new experience

▶ *Materials:* Baskets, fruit

▶ *Level:* Concrete

Facilitation

Focus: Have the children try different ways to carry fruit.

Comments/Questions: What are some ways that we carry things?

What parts of our bodies can we use?

Try walking with this basket on your head. How does it feel?

Many people in South America and Africa carry all their packages this way.

How would you carry things if you had no arms?

Variation or Extension: Carrying things using knapsacks, purses, briefcases, baskets.

WORKING IT THROUGH

Design and lay out a one-week anti-bias program plan (use Chart 9.2). Develop five activities across the required developmental domains using either the developmental-based skill approach or the theme-based approach.

Identify the areas of bias and the anti-bias skills for each activity.

Example:

Developmental-based skill	Theme-based
Seriation	Languages
Classification	Age
Problem-solving	Food

WEEKLY PLAN					
AGE: INFANT	SKILL ☐ THEME-RELATED ☐ (✓ BOX) IDENTIFY SKILL/THEME:				
	Language	**Socioemotional**	**Cognitive/ Math, Science**	**Perceptual Motor**	**Gross Motor**
Monday					
A-B AREA					
A-B SKILL					
Tuesday					
A-B AREA					
A-B SKILL					
Wednesday					
A-B AREA					
A-B SKILL					
Thursday					
A-B AREA					
A-B SKILL					
Friday					
A-B AREA					
A-B SKILL					
Dramatic/Social Play Props		Water Table Play Props		Sand Table Play Props	

CHART 9.2

Source: Hall and Rhomberg.

Appendix

HAIR ALPHABET

A — afro, auburn

B — braid, bald, bangs, bob, bun, beard, bows, barettes, balaclava, bonnet, bobby pins, blond, brunette

C — curls, cowlick, cornrows, crimped, combs

D — ducktail, dye, dandruff, dreadlocks

E — elastic bands, extensions

F — frizzy, fez, feathered, fringe

G — goatee, grey

H — hat, helmet, headdress, hijab, headband, hair net, henna, hood

K — kerchief

L — long, layered

M — mustache

N — nappy

O — oily

P — pigtails, ponytail, perm, plaits, part (side, middle)

R — ringlets, redhead, ribbons, receding, roots

S — spiked, shaven, short, sideburns, scalp, shampoo

T — toupee, topknot, tonsure, turban, toque, tangles, tousled

U — uncut, unkempt, unshaven, unisex

V — veil

W — wig, weave, wavy, whiskers

Y — yarmulke

Z — zucchetto (skullcap worn by priests, cardinals)

CHAPTER 10

Developmental-Based School-Age Activities within an Anti-Bias Framework

PURPOSE

- To enable the practitioner to explore the range of activities appropriate for school-age children within an anti-bias framework

STRATEGIES

- Designed and formatted activities that include anti-bias skills for each developmental domain relevant for the 6–12-year-old
- Explanation of the interaction process found in the "facilitation" portion of each activity
- Suggested implementation techniques to convey the anti-bias approach

MAKING THE CONNECTION

- To understand through the presentation of a completed weekly program plan, with anti-bias sections, how children can:
  1) practise anti-bias skills on a daily basis
  2) be exposed to each area of bias at least once a week

Activities for School-Age Children

The teacher's primary responsibility for this age group's affective development is to focus children's feelings on issues that require concrete action for change. Children should have many opportunities to develop critical thinking by exploring, discussing, and analyzing issues meaningful to them. At this developmental level, the affective and cognitive skills needed for pro-activism should be promoted and practised. Teachers can sustain solution-focused behaviours by acting as resources or by assisting children to obtain the necessary materials they need to achieve their goals.

The two factors of content and time frame need to be mentioned in relation to the program plan found in this chapter.

CONTENT

Ideally, a plan of experiences for school-age children should have as its source the interests of the group. In this instance, "creative expression" is a teacher-directed developmental plan used solely for the purpose of illustrating how anti-bias skills can be integrated. The activities reflect the wide variance in ages and abilities that are characteristic of a school-age program for 6–12-year-olds. In principle, support should be given to children interested in exploring such issues as sexism, racism, violence, homophobia, or any other topic related to the area of bias. The extensions for the majority of the activities are good opportunities to raise consciousness and bolster pro-activist attempts.

TIME FRAME

The program plan included is *not* a realistic schedule for one week. The amount of time devoted to projects and experiences will vary considerably depending on the issue under way and the specific group of children. The intent of the plan is to offer ideas that lend themselves to the anti-bias approach. It is apparent that the activities designed could span a month in duration.

CHART 10.1

WEEKLY PLAN					
AGE: SCHOOL AGE	SKILL ☑ THEME-RELATED ☐ (✓ BOX) IDENTIFY SKILL/THEME: CREATIVE EXPRESSION				
	Language	**Science**	**Cognitive/ Perceptual Motor**	**Creative Art**	**Gross Motor Games**
Monday	Advocacy Club	Environmentally Friendly Washing Detergents	Sewing	Backdrop Design (Natural Paints)	Seven Up— Bouncing Ball in Patterns
A-B AREA	All areas	Gender/class	Gender/culture	Gender/ability	Gender/ability/culture
A-B SKILL	Conflict resolution; group co-operation	Examine alternatives	Try anti-stereotypical activity	Group effort and cooperation	Value self-expression
Tuesday	Story Board	Greenhouse Construction and Planting	Printed Cloth	Drumming Composition	Rhyme Skipping
A-B AREA	Ability/gender/culture	Gender/culture	Culture/gender	Gender/culture/ability	All areas
A-B SKILL	Value different viewpoints; work on common goal	Try alternatives; group action	Respect each child's creativity	Group action	Anti-stereotypical experience
Wednesday	Script-writing	Making a Compost	Loom Weaving	Costume Making	Collecting Garbage
A-B AREA	Culture/ability	Class	Gender/culture	Culture/gender	Ability/gender
A-B SKILL	Develop empathy	Examine alternatives; pro-activism	Anti-stereotypical experience; examine other cultures.	Respect for others' viewpoints; pride in group effort	Pro-activism
Thursday	Dress Rehearsal	Paper Making	Lotto Matching Different Scripts	Making Props	Ti Rakau— Maori Stick Game
A-B AREA	Dependent on issue	Class/culture	Culture/ability	Gender/ability	Culture/gender
A-B SKILL	Group action for a cause	Pro-activism	Interact with diversity	Anti-stereotypical experience	Learning about other cultures
Friday	Simultaneous Signing (Theatrical Presentation)	Make Air-Freshener Potpourri	Dream Catchers	Designing a Board Game on Natural Air Cleaners	Hoop Games
A-B AREA	Dependent on issue	Class/gender/culture	Culture	All areas	Gender/ability/culture
A-B SKILL	Group action; interact with diversity	Try new alternatives	Learn about and respect another culture	Conflict resolution	Try new experience
Dramatic/Social Play Props		Water Table Play Props		Sand Table Play Props	

Source: Hall and Rhomberg.

ACTIVITY 1   Advocacy Club (Dream for a Better Future)

▶ **Age:** 6–12 years (dependent upon issue)

▶ **Curriculum Area:** Language

▶ **Curriculum Objectives:** To explore issues relating to the environment, sexism, racism, for example; to assist in developing conflict resolution and negotiation skills

▶ **Developmental Skills:** To practise making choices, taking on different viewpoints, examining alternatives, helping others

▶ **Anti-Bias Skill:** To take group action in response to identifying what is fair/unfair, moral/immoral

▶ **Materials:** Information on the issues, paper of various kinds and sizes, variety of writing utensils

▶ **Level:** Symbolic

Facilitation

Focus: Encourage self-expression and critical thinking during this brainstorming activity. Praise each child for his efforts.
Comments/Questions: How does this issue affect your life?
  How does it affect your family and friends?
Variation or Extension: Visit a landfill site; walk in the neighbourhood and identify pollution in the water, air, and land. Make and post "No Dumping" signs. Make a flyer reminding the community to recycle.

ACTIVITY 2   Story Board (Oral Storytelling of an Issue)

▶ **Age:** 6–12 years

▶ **Curriculum Area:** Language

▶ **Curriculum Objectives:** To draw pictures related to the script that will be used for the play; oral retelling using the pictures as a reference; to learn how plays are developed

▶ **Developmental Skills:** Using symbols for words; learning the art of oral storytelling; practising the ability to express emotions

▶ **Anti-Bias Skill:** To work on a common goal cooperatively; the ability to take on different viewpoints

▶ **Materials:** A variety of writing utensils and papers

▶ **Level:** Symbolic

Facilitation

Focus: Use the process of this activity to identify and work through the components of developing a story/play.
Comments/Questions: Who are the main characters?
  What are they trying to convey and how?
  How is the plot unravelling? What is the beginning, middle, climax, and conclusion?
  How do you think the story board can help you to remember the story/script?
  How is the issue being presented?
Which character is presenting the negative/positive viewpoint?
  What action can be taken to resolve the issue?
Variation or Extension: Look at cartoons (newspaper) and see how they put a skit together.

ACTIVITY 3   Scriptwriting for the Play

▶ **Age:** 6–12 years

▶ **Curriculum Area:** Language

▶ **Curriculum Objectives:** To practise printing skills; to experience other forms of writing, i.e., Braille and other languages, including signing for the title of the play and key words

▶ **Developmental Skills:** To learn about one's own and others' cultures; to work on a common goal cooperatively

▶ **Anti-Bias Skill:** To learn to respect others; to develop empathy for children who differ in abilities

▶ **Materials:** A variety of papers, writing utensils, cardboard and thumbtack to pierce Braille dots, tape recorder

▶ **Level:** Symbolic

Facilitation

Focus: Ensure that everyone gets an opportunity to speak and organize key thoughts and points. Use the tape recorder for facilitation.

Comments/Questions: This play will be presented to an audience that may include children who are hearing impaired, visually impaired, and whose first language is not English. How will you make sure that all these children understand the words and actions of your script? What will you need to do if your script partner reads only Braille?

Variation or Extension: Visit your local institute for the blind or have a volunteer come in to assist in writing Braille; invite friends from the community to help in the translation process of portions of the script.

ACTIVITY 4   Simultaneous Signing

▶ **Age:** 6–12 years

▶ **Curriculum Area:** Language

▶ **Curriculum Objectives:** To learn how to sign simple words related to the play's script

▶ **Developmental Skills:** Visual discrimination and fine-motor coordination; visual memory

▶ **Anti-Bias Skill:** To try a new experience; to help children interact comfortably with diversity

▶ **Materials:** Signing alphabet chart, dictionary, and facilitator in signing

▶ **Level:** Symbolic

Facilitation

Focus: To have each the child try spelling his or her own name, a friend's name, the title of the play.

Comments/Questions: How do you feel when you communicate with others using sign language?

Do you understand each other?

What is different from using your words?

What skills do you think hearing-impaired children need to develop?

Variation or Extension: Show a video where signing is occurring; visit a child-care centre for the hearing impaired and do a volunteer play with the hearing-impaired children.

ACTIVITY 5 # Dress Rehearsal

▶ **Age:** 6–12 years

▶ **Curriculum Area:** Language

▶ **Curriculum Objectives:** To understand the elements involved in mounting a play; to learn how to work cooperatively

▶ **Developmental Skills:** Memory; pride in group achievement

▶ **Anti-Bias Skill:** Group action for a cause

▶ **Materials:** Script, props, camcorder for replay

▶ **Level:** Symbolic

Facilitation

Focus: The process of conducting a dress rehearsal allows children to work through problems collectively. All efforts need to be praised.

Comments/Questions: How can everyone help one another?

How can you help yourself memorize the lines?

What did you like best about doing this?

What was helpful and why?

Variation or Extension: Go to a dress rehearsal at a theatre.

ACTIVITY 6 # Theatrical Presentation

▶ **Age:** 6–12 years

▶ **Curriculum Area:** Language/ Dramatics

▶ **Curriculum Objectives:** To experience putting on a theatrical performance with all the components present (i.e., music, costumes, props, and script)

▶ **Developmental Skills:** To build self-confidence; to enhance public-speaking skills; memory and sequence

▶ **Anti-Bias Skill:** Group action taken for a cause

▶ **Materials:** Props, backdrops, music, and equipment, costumes, scripts (written and signing)

▶ **Level:** Symbolic

Facilitation

Focus: This activity offers the opportunity to experience a team-building process. The pride in achieving such a goal for a particular cause can be very uplifting for a group.

Comments/Questions: How did you feel during the performance?

After?

Would you do it again?

What would you do differently next time?

Variation or Extension: Go to a young people's theatre to watch children performing.

ACTIVITY 7 — Environmentally Friendly Washing Detergents

▶ **Age:** 8–12 years

▶ **Curriculum Area:** Science

▶ **Curriculum Objectives:** To make comparisons; to analyze and draw conclusions; to practise making hypotheses and predictions

▶ **Developmental Skills:** Measuring; making decisions

▶ **Anti-Bias Skill:** To examine alternatives and to make choices

▶ **Materials:** Vinegar, pure soap, baking soda, borax, washing soda, measuring spoons, cups, mixing utensils, containers, cloths for cleaning dirty floors, cupboards, windows, and silverware

▶ **Level:** Concrete

Facilitation

Focus: To become aware that there are different ways to keep our environment clean. There exist cleaning ingredients that are environmentally friendly, inexpensive, and safer to use than the usual chemical ones for sale in stores.

Comments/Questions: Make comparisons and decide which cleaning product children would prefer to buy and why.

Variation or Extension: Visit a grocery store and examine the ingredients in and prices of similar cleaning items. Boycott products that pollute the environment by writing a letter to the manufacturer.

ACTIVITY 8 — Greenhouse Construction and Planting

▶ **Age:** 6–12 years

▶ **Curriculum Area:** Science and Woodworking

▶ **Curriculum Objectives:** To practise planning, measuring, analyzing, making predictions, group problem-solving; to learn how to use construction tools safely; to plant and care for a flower/vegetable garden

▶ **Developmental Skills:** Fine-motor and eye-hand coordination; to work cooperatively in designing and building a class greenhouse; pride in achievement

▶ **Anti-Bias Skill:** To consider different alternatives and to take group action

▶ **Materials:** Precut wood, nails, leveller, sandpaper, hammers, saws, plastic to cover greenhouse, soil, seeds, containers, gardening tools, sticks, string, watering cans. Design a watering chart and monitor growth of seeds.

▶ **Level:** Concrete and symbolic

Facilitation

Focus: This activity should enable children to explore the interrelationship between plant life and the environment, the impact of plant life on humans.

Comments/Questions: What do plants contribute to our environment?

How are they at risk?

What can we do about this on a small scale?

Variation or Extension: Visit a greenhouse in your community.

ACTIVITY 9 Making a Compost

▶ **Age:** 6–12 years

▶ **Curriculum Area:** Science

▶ **Curriculum Objectives:** To practise planning, organizing, and problem-solving skills

▶ **Developmental Skills:** To practise cooperative decision-making

▶ **Anti-Bias Skill:** To examine alternatives and take social action collectively

▶ **Materials:** Compost container, organic material, soil organisms, gloves, rakes, shovels, moisture (See your municipality's guide to backyard composting)

▶ **Level:** Concrete

Facilitation

Focus: To help children identify ways to reduce garbage for collection; to learn the process and components of composting.

Comments/Questions: What can we put in the composter?

What happens to the things we put in our composter?

What can't we put in? Why not?

How can we use the compost?

How are we going to care for it?

Who do you think should be responsible for keeping our environment clean?

What do you think the effect on the environment would be if everyone in the city composted?

Variation or Extension: Visit an ecology centre to discover other ways of composting, i.e., vermicomposting. Start composting kitchen scraps from the child-care centre.

ACTIVITY 10 Paper Making

▶ **Age:** 6–12 years

▶ **Curriculum Area:** Science

▶ **Curriculum Objectives:** Observation skills; making predictions; analyzing results

▶ **Developmental Skills:** Fine-motor coordination; sequencing; following instructions

▶ **Anti-Bias Skill:** To try a new experience and undertake a pro-active project

▶ **Materials:** Recycled newspapers, bucket, water, wire wisk, 45 mL cornstarch, 250 mL water, measuring spoons, a piece of screen about 15 cm wide, rolling pin, sheet of plastic wrap to cover screen. (See instructions in the Appendix on page 169.)

▶ **Level:** Concrete

Facilitation

Focus: Let children explore the process of making paper. Discuss the effects of manufacturing paper versus making homemade paper.

Comments/Questions: What are the difficulties of making your own paper?

How does making your own paper affect your need and use of paper?

What can we do to help the environment and society's need for paper?

Variation or Extension: Contact a local paper-saving business and start paper recycling in the school/child-care centre.

ACTIVITY 11   Making Air-Freshener Potpourri

▶ **Age:** 6–12 years

▶ **Curriculum Area:** Science

▶ **Curriculum Objectives:** Experimentation, and to practise olfactory discrimination

▶ **Developmental Skills:** To encourage creativity and foster individuality

▶ **Anti-Bias Skill:** To try new alternatives

▶ **Materials:** Baskets, small dishes, dried herbs, different spices, cinnamon sticks, orange peels, cloves in cheesecloth, etc.

▶ **Level:** Concrete

Facilitation

Focus: Children will learn how to make their own air fresheners in an environmentally friendly way and explore what effects air fresheners (that contain harsh chemicals) have on the environment, on the body.

Comments/Questions: Does your family use air fresheners?

What kind—manufactured or natural?

How does the smell of your homemade one compare to the store-bought one?

What about price?

What do you think is happening to your body when you breathe in chemicals?

What do you think may be happening to the quality of the air we are breathing?

Why do you think the Canadian government banned aerosols?

Variation or Extension: Examine ingredients of manufactured air fresheners and how they work; study the length of effectiveness between the two types of fresheners and discuss conclusions.

ACTIVITY 12   Sewing

▶ **Age:** 6–12 years

▶ **Curriculum Area:** Perceptual motor

▶ **Curriculum Objectives:** To improve eye-hand coordination; to develop self-help skills

▶ **Developmental Skills:** To increase problem-solving; pride in accomplishment of a project

▶ **Anti-Bias Skill:** To try an anti-stereotypical activity; to explore similarities and differences of one activity in other cultures

▶ **Materials:** Clothes for mending or a variety of patterned and coloured fabrics, steel needles, wood and bone needles from aboriginal cultures, scissors, threads (sewing machine is optional)

▶ **Level:** Concrete

Facilitation

Focus: Discussion on the need for boys and girls to learn sewing; brief exploration on the history of sewing and usage of implements.

Comments/Questions: Who sews in your family? (gender related)

What kinds of material are your clothes made of?

What kinds of stitching are used?

What kind of needles were used before the use of metals?

Variation or Extension: Visit a sewing shop and discover all the different tools available for mending and sewing. Compare prices of fabrics and select some for the next day's creative activity.

ACTIVITY 13 Printed Cloth

▶ **Age:** 6–12 years

▶ **Curriculum Area:** Perceptual motor

▶ **Curriculum Objectives:** To practise fine-motor coordination; spatial design; individual creativity

▶ **Developmental Skills:** Cause and effect; following instructions in a sequence

▶ **Anti-Bias Skill:** To learn about another culture; to respect each child's creativity

▶ **Materials:** Plain fabric (solid colours), scissors, spools, bottle caps, small cookie cutters, corks, vegetables with designs cut out, dry tempera paint, water, and paper towels (see instruc-

tions in the Appendix, page 169)

▶ **Level:** Concrete

Facilitation

Focus: To enable the children to experience the process of making prints on cloth and learn about cultures that practise this process.
Comments/Questions: What kinds of prints are on your clothing?
   Ashanti people of Ghana painted and stamped patterns on fabrics used for garments, as do people in Thailand, Central America, etc.
Variation or Extension: Books on cloth making around the world; books on batiking.

ACTIVITY 14 Loom Weaving

▶ **Age:** 6–12 years

▶ **Curriculum Area:** Perceptual motor

▶ **Curriculum Objectives:** To experiment making patterns and designs; fine-motor coordination

▶ **Developmental Skills:** To follow a sequence in a process; an opportunity to explore creativity and individuality

▶ **Anti-Bias Skill:** To participate in an anti-stereotypical experience; to learn about one's own and other cultures

▶ **Materials:** Different types of yarns, wooden looms (individual sized and/or a large

one for group project), scissors

▶ **Level:** Concrete

Facilitation

Focus: To learn how to weave yarn through the loom in order to produce cloth.
Comments/Questions: Examine material of your own clothing in comparison to material woven on a loom. Discuss differences and experiment with patterns in the weaving process; discuss types of looms different cultures use.
Variation or Extension: Visit a historical centre and explore weaving and loom demonstrations.

ACTIVITY 15 Lotto Matching Different Scripts

▶ **Age:** 8–12 years

▶ **Curriculum Area:** Perceptual motor

▶ **Curriculum Objectives:** To match similar scripts and learn how to pronounce the sounds of depicted letters/phrases

▶ **Developmental Skills:** Visual and auditory discrimination; to make comparisons; to support literacy

▶ **Anti-Bias Skill:** To foster awareness of other cultures; to interact with diversity

▶ **Materials:** Lotto cards with different letters or phrases printed on them, game boards

▶ **Level:** Representational and Symbolic

Facilitation

Focus: Exploration and familiarization with different language scripts.

Comments/Questions: What languages do you speak?

What languages do your family/friends speak? and read?

Where does your family come from?

Ask parents for assistance in the writing and pronunciation of phrases.

Variation or Extension: Have visitors come in and talk about their language.

ACTIVITY 16 Dream Catchers

▶ **Age:** 6–12 years

▶ **Curriculum Area:** Perceptual motor

▶ **Curriculum Objectives:** Eye-hand coordination; spatial sequencing

▶ **Developmental Skills:** Individual creativity; listening and responding

▶ **Anti-Bias Skill:** To learn and respect another culture

▶ **Materials:** Willow branch, leather straps, string, waxed dental floss, scissors, feathers, beads, leather string (see instructions in the Appendix, page 169)

▶ **Level:** Concrete

Facilitation

Focus: To learn the significance of dream catchers in the native culture and to design individual ones.

Comments/Questions: Can you guess what a dream catcher is?

For whom do you think dream catchers were made?

Discuss the significance of a dream catcher to native beliefs and traditions.

Variation or Extension: Visit a native friendship centre and learn about other cultural traditions of the First Nations people.

ACTIVITY 17 # Backdrop Design (Natural Paints)

▶ **Age:** 6–12 years

▶ **Curriculum Area:** Creative

▶ **Curriculum Objectives:** Creative self-expression; fine-motor coordination; to encourage the use of tools other than brushes

▶ **Developmental Skills:** To practise group planning; organizing; problem-solving

▶ **Anti-Bias Skill:** To recognize the importance of everyone's contribution to a group effort

▶ **Materials:** Natural paints (see instructions in Appendix, page 169), cloth paper, large, plain paper, rolled paper, corrugated cardboard, brushes in a variety of sizes, rollers, feathers, and scissors

▶ **Level:** Concrete

Facilitation

Focus: This activity enables children to listen and work cooperatively in assessing what they would like to see as a backdrop to their play. If they are having problems, let them draw ideas on smaller paper initially and then collectively decide which ideas can be pooled and reproduced in a larger format.

Comments/Questions: Prompt children to think about the key points in their play that would require support; help them to think through all the steps required for this process.

Variation or Extension: Visit a theatre and look at backdrops.

ACTIVITY 18 # Drumming Composition

▶ **Age:** 9–12 years

▶ **Curriculum Area:** Creative

▶ **Curriculum Objectives:** Fine-motor coordination; individual creativity in drum making and composition; to plan rhythms

▶ **Developmental Skills:** To discover patterns; auditory memory; group problem-solving

▶ **Anti-Bias Skill:** To work respectfully with others on a group project

▶ **Materials:** Tape recorder, blank tapes, different-sized and -shaped waste baskets, tin barrel, plastic boxes, collage materials, markers, glue, and scissors

▶ **Level:** Concrete

Facilitation

Focus: To give the children an opportunity to work collectively; to compose musical sounds in accompaniment to the play; to compose patterns for drumbeats and analyze tempo needs; to practise the music with the storyboard and assess how it matches.

Comments/Questions: What were some of the problems to work through as you were composing your own music?

How does it feel when you hear it recorded?

Variation or Extension: Obtain tapes of different drumming groups, i.e., Caribbean, South Pacific, African, and North American.

ACTIVITY 19 ## Costume Making

▶ **Age:** 6–12 years

▶ **Curriculum Area:** Creative

▶ **Curriculum Objectives:** Creative expression; decision-making; working with a variety of materials

▶ **Developmental Skills:** To improve fine-motor coordination; planning and organizational skills

▶ **Anti-Bias Skill:** To promote group cooperation and respect for one another's viewpoints

▶ **Materials:** Printed cloth made by the children, elastic, fabric, Velcro, buttons, snaps, beads, ribbons, sequins, lace, feathers, glue, needles, threads, scissors, cardboard, etc.

▶ **Level:** Concrete

Facilitation

Focus: This activity allows individual children to design and create a costume that supports their character in the play. Assist them to think about the script and the characters when planning the costumes.

Comments/Questions: What mood or idea do you want the costume to convey?

Is it stereotypical? Why or why not?

How does your costume match your character?

What accessories do you think you might want to add?

Variation or Extension: Have someone from a costume store visit the class with samples for the children to try on and explore.

ACTIVITY 20 ## Making Props

▶ **Age:** 6–12 years

▶ **Curriculum Area:** Creative

▶ **Curriculum Objectives:** Creative expression in the use of diverse materials and tools; to promote a sense of aesthetic design

▶ **Developmental Skills:** To practise problem-solving; planning; organization; measurement; to learn safety rules when working with construction materials

▶ **Anti-Bias Skill:** To engage in an anti-stereotypical experience; to work cooperatively on a group project; to recognize one's own and others' talents

▶ **Materials:** Use natural paints (see Appendix, page 169), wood, hammer, nails, sandpaper, saw, boxes of differing sizes, bristol board, cloth paper, brushes of varying types, crayons, markers, plastic containers, string, scissors, glue, tape, etc.

▶ **Level:** Concrete

Facilitation

Focus: Assist the children as they explore the use of a variety of construction materials to design and make props for the theatrical presentation. Facilitate blueprint designing if need be, and then support group organization around who wants to create what.

Comments/Questions: What are the numerous ways you could use these materials in order to design props?

How can you make this prop taller? wider? more stable?

How can you make the stage look less cluttered?

What prop gives you the mood you want to convey?

Variation or Extension: Visit a woodworking shop and focus on how carpenters measure and assemble wood pieces.

ACTIVITY 21

Designing a Board Game on Natural Air Cleaners

▶ **Age:** 6–12 years

▶ **Curriculum Area:** Creative

▶ **Curriculum Objectives:** To provide the opportunity to design a board game; to promote the ability to create rules, either competitive or cooperative in nature

▶ **Developmental Skills:** To improve making decisions; visual discrimination; sequencing; problem-solving

▶ **Anti-Bias Skill:** Conflict resolution; listening to others' viewpoints

▶ **Materials:** Environmentally friendly plastic, and access to an oven to create movable pieces, cardboard for base, multicoloured paper, markers, crayons, dice, spinner, fastener, scissors, glue, photocopied pictures of plants that are natural air cleaners, e.g., spider plant, English ivy, golden pothos, aloe vera, etc.

▶ **Level:** Concrete and Representational

Facilitation

Focus: This activity allows a group effort to design and create a board game that involves learning about house plants and the role they play in keeping the air we breathe clean. Provide other board games to analyze for rules, pieces, and general design. Discuss what natural air cleaners are and what they do. Discuss the problem of indoor air pollution.

Comments/Questions: Was it difficult deciding on the type of game you were going to make?

If there were problems, how did you work them through?

Variation or Extension: Have the group select the best game and together compose a marketing proposal. Send it to various toy companies.

ACTIVITY 22

Seven Up—Bouncing Ball in Patterns

▶ **Age:** 6–12 years

▶ **Curriculum Area:** Motor/Games

▶ **Curriculum Objectives:** To coordinate using physical and verbal skills simultaneously; to practise balance and motor coordination

▶ **Developmental Skills:** Creative self-expression; memory

▶ **Anti-Bias Skill:** Valuing individual self-expression and that of others

▶ **Materials:** Balls of various sizes for differing levels of challenge; words to rhyme; researched chants in other languages

▶ **Level:** Concrete

Facilitation

Focus: To give children the opportunity to practise bouncing balls in a pattern while they chant a rhyme. Demonstrate the game and practise rhymes in small circles. Let the children practise to their own level of ability. Once the children feel the game is mastered, teams could be set up for additional challenges.

Comments/Questions: How did you decide on your pattern and your rhyme?

How could you play this game if you had no arms?

If you were blind?

Do girls bounce the balls differently than boys?

Variation or Extension: Discover other ball games with rhymes.

ACTIVITY 23 Rhyme Skipping

▶ **Age:** 6–12 years

▶ **Curriculum Area:** Motor/Games

▶ **Curriculum Objectives:** Large-motor coordination required for skipping; projectile management; spatial relations

▶ **Developmental Skills:** Turn taking; to learn old and new language patterns for skipping

▶ **Anti-Bias Skill:** To try an anti-stereotypical activity

▶ **Materials:** Individual skipping ropes, group ropes (single and double); chants and rhymes

▶ **Level:** Concrete and Symbolic

Facilitation

Focus: Discuss how skipping has become a competitive sport and how famous athletes use skipping to develop their large-muscle skills.

Comments/Questions: Is it easier or harder to skip with the rhymes?

Which ones did you find the most challenging and why?

Who do you think likes to skip?

Variation or Extension: Join a skip-a-thon and let the children select a charity for which they will raise funds.

ACTIVITY 24 Collecting Garbage in Your Neighbourhood

▶ **Age:** 6–12 years

▶ **Curriculum Area:** Motor/Games

▶ **Curriculum Objectives:** Large-muscle development; balance; motor coordination

▶ **Developmental Skills:** To identify environmental pollution; classification by type; mapping and charting

▶ **Anti-Bias Skill:** To become pro-active in your neighbourhood

▶ **Materials:** Bags for collection, map of neighbourhood, graph paper, and markers

▶ **Level:** Concrete, Representational, and Symbolic

Facilitation

Focus: To examine our environment and assist in cleaning it by collecting re-usable items.

Comments/Questions: What do you think the garbage found in our neighbourhood does to the environment?

How do you feel when you see such pollution in your community?

How can we make a difference with this problem?

Let's group the objects you collected. What do people seem to throw out the most? the least?

What does the most damage to the earth? Which streets had the most garbage?

Variation or Extension: Chart the areas that had the most garbage pollution; write a letter to a local politician to encourage recycling in that area.

ACTIVITY 25 Ti Rakau—Maori Stick Game

▶ *Age:* 8–12 years

▶ *Curriculum Area:* Motor/Games

▶ *Curriculum Objectives:* To practise eye-hand coordination, balance; spatial relations

▶ *Developmental Skills:* Experiencing rhythms in a group game; to enhance quick reaction; to work in partnership

▶ *Anti-Bias Skill:* To become familiar with another culture

▶ *Materials:* Dowels and songs

▶ *Level:* Concrete

Facilitation

Focus: To have the children learn a new game involving rhythms and patterns. Assign children partners by counting off and positioning them in two horizontal rows. Let children practise gently throwing the sticks sideways and forward to partners in time to the tapping sticks and song.

Comments/Questions: Did you find the game easy to do?

Why?

Why not?

What did it teach you about working with partners?

Variation or Extension: Discover other stick games with patterns.

ACTIVITY 26 Hoop Games

▶ *Age:* 6–12 years

▶ *Curriculum Area:* Motor/Games

▶ *Curriculum Objectives:* To practise eye-hand coordination and targeting skills; body control and balance

▶ *Developmental Skills:* Sense of accomplishment; turn taking

▶ *Anti-Bias Skill:* To try a new experience that is common to other cultures

▶ *Materials:* Hula hoops, sticks, dowels, bean bags, balls

▶ *Level:* Concrete

Facilitation

Focus: To have children learn how to roll a hoop with a stick. Discuss the history of hoop games, i.e., native people, Inuit, European, and African peoples.

Comments/Questions: After practice ask the children what they liked about this game.

Why do they think it was used by hunting peoples (Northern) as a teaching tool for their children?

Variation or Extension: Explore other hoop-related games. Sing rhymes while playing.

WORKING IT THROUGH

Design and lay out a one-week anti-bias program plan (use Chart 10.2). Develop five activities across the required developmental domains using either the developmental-based skill approach or the theme-based approach.

Identify the areas of bias and the anti-bias skills for each activity.

Example:

Development-based skill	*Theme-based*
Evaluation	Music
Comparison	School bullies
Activism	Recycling

CHART 10.2

WEEKLY PLAN

AGE: INFANT	SKILL ☐ THEME-RELATED ☐ (✓ BOX) IDENTIFY SKILL/THEME:				
	Language	Socioemotional	Cognitive/ Perceptual Motor	Creative Art	Gross Motor Games
Monday					
A-B AREA					
A-B SKILL					
Tuesday					
A-B AREA					
A-B SKILL					
Wednesday					
A-B AREA					
A-B SKILL					
Thursday					
A-B AREA					
A-B SKILL					
Friday					
A-B AREA					
A-B SKILL					
Dramatic/Social Play Props		Water Table Play Props		Sand Table Play Props	

Source: Hall and Rhomberg.

Appendix

PAPER MAKING (POLLUTION PROBE, 1991, 192):

1. Tear newspapers into shreds and place in bucket to the halfway mark.

2. Add water, wetting the pieces thoroughly. Let stand for two hours.

3. Beat mixture into a creamy pulp with the wire whisk.

4. Dissolve the cornstarch in water and add to the pulp mixture. Mix again.

5. Submerge piece of screen in pulp and extract. Repeat this procedure until the screen has a layer of pulp about 3 mm thick.

6. Spread out newspapers and lay the pulp-covered screen on the sheets.

7. Cover the screen with plastic wrap. Press out excess water with a rolling pin. Set the screen up so air can dry the pulp.

8. When the pulp is dry, gently peel the recycled paper off the screen.

Variation: You could add small pieces of coloured thread to step 5 and produce decorative paper.

PRINTED CLOTH (ALLEN ET AL., 1992, 9):

To make the printing pads, place folded wet paper towels in a shallow dish and sprinkle each with 15 mL of dry tempera paint. Let it sit until paint becomes moist. Children can then press items on pads and use them to print designs on fabric.

DREAM CATCHERS (ALLEN ET AL., 1992, 49):

Shape a willow branch into a circle and secure with a leather strap. Weave dental floss in and out and across the circle to make a web. Attach feathers and beads at the bottom. Attach leather string to the top for hanging.

NATURAL PAINTS (KOHL AND GARNER, *GOOD EARTH ART*, 188):

Materials: juice boiled off from vegetables/fruit (e.g., carrot, spinach, beets, onion, blueberries) plus 1/2 cup finely chopped soap chips, 1 cup cornstarch, 6 cups water, large saucepan, coloured chalks crushed (if not using natural juice dyes), storage containers with lids.

Combine soap chips, cornstarch, and water in pan; bring mixture to boil over medium heat, stirring constantly. Remove when mixture has thickened. Pour into individual containers and if not using juice then place one colour of crushed chalk in each container and mix while still warm. Let cool before storing in covered containers.

Try other textures and scents, i.e., coffee, vanilla, cinnamon.

CHAPTER 11

Resources

CANADIAN RESOURCES

- Training resources
- Journals and papers
- Teacher resources
- Teaching materials, equipment, and books
- Children's publishers
- Toy fairs

AMERICAN RESOURCES

- Training resources
- Teacher resources
- Teaching materials

INTERNATIONAL RESOURCES

- Teacher resources

FURTHER READINGS

- Canadian
- American
- International

Canadian Resources

TRAINING RESOURCES

Biocchi, Roseanne, and Shanthi Radcliffe
  1983. *A Shared Experience: Bridging Cultures—Resources for Cross Cultural Training.* London, ON: London Cross Cultural Learner Centre.

Clarke, D., C. Holman, K. Swinburne, and T. Tunnacliffe
  1992. *Family Day Care Training for Second Language Learners.* Ottawa, ON: Andrew Fleck Child Care Services.

Congress of Black Women
  1992. *Children Are Not the Problem.* Anti-racist child care strategies film. CCIF Project. Toronto, ON: Congress of Black Women.

Council for Yukon Indians
  1991. *Cross Cultural Strategies. Background Information for Teachers of First Nations Students.* Whitehorse, NWT: Council for Yukon Indians.

Early Childhood Multicultural Services
  1992. *Educating Young Children in a Multicultural Society. An Introduction to Goals, Strategies and Resources.* Video. Vancouver, BC: Early Childhood Multicultural Services.

Meadow Lake/University of Victoria
  1989–93. *Indian Child Care Education and Career Ladder.* CCIF Project #4776-08-89/009. Meadow Lake, BC: Meadow Lake Tribal Council.

Mock, Karen
  1988. *Race Relations Training: A Manual and Resource Guide for Practitioners and Consultants.* Race Relations Directorate. Toronto, ON: Ontario Ministry of Citizenship.

Multiculturalism Canada
  1985. *Cross-Cultural Awareness Education and Training for Professionals—A Manual.* Ottawa, ON: Multiculturalism Canada.

Murphy Kilbride, Kenise
  1990. *Multicultural Early Childhood Education Facilitator's Manual.* Toronto, ON: Ryerson Polytechnic Institute.

Ontario Ministry of Community and Social Services
  1990. *Families and Teachers: Partners for Children.* Video. Toronto, ON: Ministry of Community and Social Services.

Umar, Hammda, and Cross-Cultural Parenting Committee
1989. *Cross-Cultural Parenting Programs—Training Manual*. Calgary, AB: Immigrant Women's Centre.

Union of Ontario Indians
1989. *Anishinabek Early Childhood Education Project*. CCIF Project #4776-06-89/001. North Bay, ON: Union of Ontario Indians.

JOURNALS AND PAPERS

Christensen, Carole Pigler
1993. "Cross-Cultural Awareness: A Developmental Process in a Multicultural and Multiracial Society." Paper prepared for the Canadian Council for Multicultural and Intercultural Education (CCMIE), Fifth National Conference on Multicultural/Intercultural and Race Relations Education, Vancouver, BC: November.

Multiculturalism—A triennial publication of the Canadian Council for Multicultural and Intercultural Education, in association with Multiculturalism and Education, Faculty of Education, University of Toronto.
ECE issue: Vol. V, 4 (1982).
Special ECE issue: Vol. XIV, 2/3 (1992).
Vol. XV, 2/3 (1993).

TESL Canada Journal. A journal devoted to teaching English as a second language.

Together. Newsletter from Multiculturalism and Citizenship Canada. Ottawa, ON.

TEACHER RESOURCES

Bailey, Cindy
1993. *Start-Up Multiculturalism. Integrate the Canadian Cultural Reality in Your Classroom*. Markham, ON: Pembroke Publishers.

B'nai Brith
1987. *Teacher, They Call Me a ————. Prejudice and Discrimination in the Classroom*. New York and Toronto: Anti-Defamation League of B'nai Brith.

Bordy, Ed, et al., eds.
1993. *Spinning Tales, Weaving Hope: Stories of Peace, Justice and the Environment*. Gabriola, BC: New Society Publishing.

Bowers, Vivien, and Diane Swanson
1989. *More Than Meets the Eye: Student Book*. Faculty of Education, University of British Columbia. Vancouver, BC: Pacific Education Press.

Brodey, Kim, and Jerry Brodey
1992. *Can You Hear My Voice: Anti-Bias Songs and Classroom Activities for Kindergarten through Grade 6*. Audiotape and Teacher's Activity Guide. Toronto, ON: Kim and Jerry Brodey Productions.

Bruchac, Joseph
1991. *The Native Stories from Keepers of the Earth*. Saskatoon, SK: Fifth House Publishers.

Caduto, Michael, and Joseph Bruchac
1989. *Keepers of the Earth: Native Stories and Environmental Activities for Children*. Saskatoon, SK: Fifth House Publishers.

———.
1991. *Keepers of the Animals: Native Stories and Wildlife Activities for Children*. Saskatoon, SK: Fifth House Publishers.

———.
1994. *Keepers of the Night: Native Stories and Nocturnal Activities for Children*. Saskatoon, SK: Fifth House Publishers.

Cech, Maureen
1990. *Globalchild: Multicultural Resources for Young Children*. Ottawa, ON: Global Child.

Council for Yukon Indians
1988. *Curriculum and Program Requirements for Day Care Centre Based on Traditional Yukon Indian Culture*. CCIF Project #4775-12-88/001. Whitehorse, NWT: Council for Yukon Indians.

Fralick, Paul
1989. *Make It Multicultural—Musical Activities for Early Childhood Education*. Hamilton, ON: Mohawk College.

Gagnon, Andre, and Anne Gagnon, eds.
1988. *Canadian Books for Young Children*, 4th ed. Toronto, ON: University of Toronto.

Graeme, Jocelyn, and Ruth Fahlman
1990. *Hand in Hand—Multicultural Experiences for Young Children*. Curriculum Series for Preschool to Grade 3. Don Mills, ON: Addison-Wesley.

Grant, Agnes, ed.
1992. *Our Bit of Truth: An Anthology of Canadian Native Literature*. Winnipeg, MB: Pemmican Publications.

Greenspoon, Bayla
1992. *Festivals of Light Resource Package*. Vancouver, BC: Early Childhood Multicultural Services.

————.

 1993. "Diversity." Audiotape for children. Vancouver, BC: Early Childhood Multicultural Services.

Grevious, S. Clark
 1993. *Ready to Use Multicultural Activities for Primary Children*. Scarborough, ON: Prentice Hall Canada.

Jobe, Ron
 1993. *Cultural Connections: Using Literature to Explore World Cultures with Children*. Markham, ON: Pembroke Publishers.

Micmac Early Childhood Resource Centre, Nova Scotia.

Parry, Caroline
 1987. *Let's Celebrate! Canada's Special Days*. Toronto, ON: Kids Can Press.

Petrie, Monica
 1992. *Annotated Bibliography of 100 Multicultural Books for Young Children*. Vancouver, BC: Early Childhood Multicultural Services.

Rogers, Vicki
 1990a. *Apple's Not the Only Pie. A Multicultural Storybook*. Faculty of Education, University of British Columbia. Vancouver, BC: Pacific Education Press.

————.

 1990b. *All the Colours of the Rainbow. A Teacher's Guide*. Faculty of Education, University of British Columbia. Vancouver, BC: Pacific Education Press.

Sawyer, Don, and Wayne Lundeberg
 1993. *The NESA Activities Handbook for Native and Multicultural Classrooms*, Vol. 3. Vancouver, BC: Arsenal Pulp Press.

Toronto Board of Education
 1991. *Anti-Racist Education and the Adult Learner: A Handbook for Educators in Adult and Continuing Education*. Toronto, ON: Toronto Board of Education.

University of British Columbia
 1992. *Folk Rhymes from Around the World. Racial Harmony through Education*. Faculty of Education, University of British Columbia. Vancouver, BC: Pacific Education Press.

Williams, Lorna, and Mary Longman
 1991. *SIMA 7 Come and Join Me*. Faculty of Education, University of British Columbia. Vancouver, BC: Pacific Educational Press.

TEACHING MATERIALS, EQUIPMENT, AND BOOKS

Canplay
Division of Nichigan (Canada)
875 Wilson Road South, Unit 2
Oshawa, ON L1H 8B1
(905) 576-3311
Fax (905) 433-1866

Friendimals—a line of plush stuffed animals that represent endangered species: orangutan, panda, eagle, manatee, seal, polar bear, timber wolf, and elephant. Each comes with a nametag, printed storybook telling about the species, its location on a world map, canvas carry bag, cassette with song, and a detachable teardrop.

Childscope
91 Armstrong Avenue
Georgetown, ON L7G 4S1
1-800-668-4302
Fax (905) 873-2955

This catalogue service offers a wide variety of multicultural puzzles as well as nonsexist occupational puzzles.

Cross Cultural Communication Centre
2909 Dundas Street West
Toronto, ON M6P 1Z1
(416) 760-7855

This community-education and resource centre is committed to developing programs and materials on anti-racism, multiculturalism, immigration, immigrant women, refugees, and community development. A catalogue describing services and materials is available.

Early Childhood Multicultural Services (E.C.M.S.)
#201-1675 West 4th Avenue
Vancouver, BC V6J 1L8
(604) 739-9456
Fax (604) 739-3289

Posters, pamphlets, books, and other professional-development resource materials are available.

Fireplay Books Catalogue
250 Sparks Avenue
Willowdale, ON M2H 2S4
(416) 499-8412
Fax (416) 499-8313

A resource for calendars with exquisite photographs of Canadian people and art.

Native Council of Canada
384 Bank Street, Second Floor
Ottawa, ON K2P 1Y4

Parentbooks
201 Harbord Street
Toronto, ON M5S 1H6
(416) 537-8334
Fax (416) 537-9499

This bookstore carries over 10 000 titles of interest to parents, teachers, and training institutions. Bibliographies on affective, anti-racist, and cross-cultural education and many other topics are available.

Roylco
30 Northland Road
Waterloo, ON N2V 1Y1
(519) 885-0451
Fax (519) 885-3251

Multicultural and multiracial resource material, arts and crafts with people-coloured felt, hair-coloured yarn, people-coloured cloth pins, sponge people.

Snailbrush
7668 Settler's Way
North Gower, ON K0A 2T0
(613) 258-7491
Fax (613) 258-4833

This toy manufacturer has a wonderful array of multiethnic dolls which come in 14 different skin colours, with a range of facial features and hair styles. Of special note are the special-needs dolls with a wide range of medical conditions, such as dolls with hearing aids, with a white cane, amputees with crutches, a doll wearing a leg brace, and one in a wheelchair. Personal requests for dolls with a special need (e.g., Down's syndrome) can be filled.

Specially written nonviolent fairy tales, with a multiracial cast of characters who show that children can make a difference, are also available.

Tree Huggers
501 Palmerston Boulevard
Toronto, ON M6G 2P2
(416) 516-8444
Fax (416) 516-1956

Treehuggers are huggable, machine-washable, cloth multiracial dolls. Outfits come with shoelaces, apron strings, buttons, and zippers. There are also tree seeds in the pocket of each wildlife apron with instructions for planting, for an additional environmental message.

Wintergreen
14 Connie Crescent, Unit 10
Concord, ON L4K 2W8
(905) 669-2815

1-800-268-1268
Fax 1-800-567-8054
Fax (905) 669-2481

A wide selection of multiethnic dolls with accurate features and skin colours are available. Doll clothing is unisex and nonstereotypical. New for 1994 are differently abled dolls complete with specialized equipment such as a walker, guide dog, harness and cane, leg braces and forearm crutches, and a wheelchair. Dramatic play props include foods and a superb assortment of breads from around the world.

CHILDREN'S PUBLISHERS

Annick Press
15 Patrick Avenue
Willowdale, ON M2M 1H9
(416) 221-4802
Fax (416) 221-8400

This publishing house has been committed to producing innovative, humorous, and thought-provoking children's literature. The publishers have taken on the responsibility of depicting children who respect themselves and others, and who accept differences without fear. Books from this publishing house consistently meet the goals of the anti-bias approach. They also offer an excellent selection of toddler board books designed in the same spirit.

Canadian Children's Book Centre
35 Spadina Road
Toronto, ON M5R 2S9
(416) 975-0010

This is a national, nonprofit organization established in 1976 to promote the reading, writing, and illustrating of Canadian children's books. The centre produces and distributes information about Canadian authors, children's titles, and many other services. Catalogues on Canadian Multicultural Books for Young Children are a rich resource of titles ranging from preschoolers to teens.

Kids Can Press
29 Birch Avenue
Toronto, ON M4V 1E2
(416) 925-5437
Fax (416) 960-5437

This publisher produces a wide assortment of fiction, crafts, nature and science, picture, and information books that cater to a varied audience. The majority of the content is Canadian.

TOY FAIRS

Toy fairs are an excellent source of new ideas for teachers. The list below is a partial one.

Canadian Toy and Decoration Fair (generally held in January, in Toronto, ON)
Contact:
Canadian Toy Manufacturers Association
P.O. Box 294
Kleinburg, ON L0J 1C0
(416) 893-1689
Fax (416) 893-2392

Canadian Toy Importers Fair
Contact:
Canadian Toy Importers Association
32 Carluke Crescent, Suite 510
Willowdale, ON M2L 2J3
(416) 225-4419

One of a Kind Canadian Craft Show and Sale
(usually held in Toronto, ON, Automotive Building at Exhibition Place)
Contact:
The Canadian Craft Show Ltd.
21 Grenville Street
Toronto, ON M4Y 1A1
(416) 960-3680

American Resources

TRAINING RESOURCES

The Australian Early Childhood Association
"We All Belong: Multicultural Child Care That Works." Training video. Distributed by Redleaf Press, St. Paul, MN.

Baker, Gwendolyn C.
1983. *Planning and Organizing for Multicultural Instruction*. Reading, PA: Addison-Wesley.

Beginning Equal Project
1983. *Beginning Equal: A Manual about Non-Sexist Childrearing for Infants and Toddlers*. New York: Women's Action Alliance and Pre-School Association.

Grant, C., and C. Sleeter
1989. *Turning on Learning: Five Approaches for Multicultural Teaching Plans for Race, Class, Gender and Disability*. Columbus, OH: Merrill.

Hernandez, Hilda
> 1989. *Multicultural Education: A Teacher's Guide to Content and Process*. Columbus, OH: Merrill.

Williams, L., Y. De Gaetano, C. Harrington, and I. Sutherland
> 1985. *Alerta: A Multicultural, Bilingual Approach to Teaching Young Children*. Menlo Park, CA: Addison-Wesley.

York, Stacey
> 1992. *Developing Roots and Wings. A Trainer's Guide to Affirming Culture in Early Childhood Programs*. St. Paul, MN: Redleaf Press.

TEACHER RESOURCES

Abbott, M., and B. Polk
> 1993. *Celebrating Our Diversity: Using Multicultural Literature to Promote Cultural Awareness*. Carthage, IL: Fearon Teacher Aids.

Froschl, M., L. Colon, E. Rubin, and B. Sprung
> 1984. *Including All of Us: An Early Childhood Curriculum about Disabilities*. New York: Educational Equity Concepts.

Hopkins, S., and J. Winters, eds.
> 1990. *Discover the World: Empowering Children to Value Themselves, Others and the Earth*. Philadelphia, PA: New Society Publishers.

Hopson, D.P., and D.S. Hopson
> 1993. *Raising the Rainbow Generation: Teaching Your Children to Be Successful in a Multicultural Society*. New York: Simon and Schuster.

Jones, Bessie, and Bessie Lomax Hawes
> 1972. *Step It Down: Games, Plays, Songs and Stories from the Afro-American Heritage*. Athens, GA: University of Georgia.

McNeill, E., V. Schmidt, and J. Allen
> 1981. *Cultural Awareness for Young Children*. Dallas, TX: The Learning Tree.

Meagher, Laura
> 1991. *Teaching Children about Global Awareness*. New York: Crossroads.

Milord, Susan
> 1992. *Hands around the World: 365 Creative Ways to Build Cultural Awareness and Global Respect*. Charlotte, VT: Williamson Publishing.

Nelson, Wayne, and Henry Glass
> 1992. *International Playtime: Classroom Games and Dances from around the World*. Carthage, IL: Fearon Teacher Aids.

Ryan, Margaret
    1989. *Cultural Journeys: 84 Art and Social Science Activities from around the World*. Holmes Beach, FL: Learning Publishing.

Schniedewind, Nancy, and Ellen Davidson
    1983. *Open Minds to Equality: A Sourcebook of Learning Activities to Promote Race, Sex, Class and Age Equity*. Englewood Cliffs, NJ: Prentice Hall.

Schuman, Jo Miles
    1981. *Art from Many Hands*. Worcester, MA: Davis Publications.

Spiegelman, Art
    (Reprinted 1986). *Maus: A Survivor's Tale*. 2 vols. New York: Pantheon Books.

Terzian, Alexandra
    1993. *The Kids' Multicultural Art Book: Art and Craft Experiences from around the World*. Charlotte, VT: Williamson Publishing.

Thompson, Barbara
    1993. *Words Can Hurt You: Beginning a Program of Anti-Bias Education*. Menlo Park, CA: Addison-Wesley.

Walker, Barbara
    1992. *Laughing Together: Giggles and Grins from around the Globe*. Minneapolis, MN: Free Spirit Press.

Yolen, Jane, ed.
    1992. *Street Rhymes around the World*. Honesdale, PA: Boyds Mills Press.

TEACHING MATERIALS

Afro-American Publishing Company
819 Wabash Avenue, South
Chicago, IL 60605
(312) 922-1147

American Indian Resource Center
6518 Miles Avenue
Huntington Park, CA 90255
(213) 583-1461

The Braille Book Club
National Braille Press
88 St. Stephen Street
Boston, MA 02115
Dual-track books available
(617) 266-6160

Childcraft
20 Kilmer Road
P.O. Box 3081
Edison, NJ 08818
1-800-631-5652

Council on Interracial Books for Children
1841 Broadway
New York, NY 10023
(212) 757-5339

Cultural Links: A Multicultural Resource Guide
Multicultural Project for Communication and Education
186 Lincoln Street
Boston, MA 02111

Education Equity Concepts
114 East 32nd Street
New York, NY
(212) 725-1803

Information Centre on Children's Cultures
United States Committee for UNICEF
331 East 38th Street
New York, NY 10016
(212) 686-5522

Institute for Peace and Justice
4144 Lindell, Room 122
St. Louis, MO 63108
(314) 533-4445

National Black Child Development Institute
11023 15th Street N.W., Suite 600
Washington, DC 20005
(202) 387-1281

Native American Research Information Service
University of Oklahoma
555 Constitution Street, Room 237
Norman, OK 73037

United Indians of All Tribes Foundation
Community Education Services
Discovery Park
P.O. Box 99100
Seattle, WA 98199
(206) 285-4425

Women's Educational Equity Act Publishing Center
Education Development Center
55 Chapel Street, Suite 200
Newton, MA 02160
1-800-225-3088

International Resources

TEACHER RESOURCES

ENGLAND

Development Education Centre
(for anti-racism training resources)
998 Bristol Road
Selly Oaks
Birmingham B29 6LE
021-472-3255

Soma Books
38 Kennington Lane
London SE11 4LS
071-735-2101

Tamarind
Child's Play
Ashworth Road
Bridgemead
Swindon SN5 7YD
079-361-6286

Working Group Against Racism in Children's Resources
460 Wandsworth Road
London SW8 3LX

AUSTRALIA

Ethnic Child Care Development Unit
142 Addison Road, Hut 13
Marrickville, N.S.W.
2204 Australia
(03) 569-1288

Free Kindergarten Association
Multicultural Resource Centre

273 Church Street, 1st Floor
Richmond
3121 Victoria
(03) 428-4471

Multicultural Resource Unit
Lady Gowrie Child Centre
Elliott Avenue
Erskineville, N.S.W.
2034 Australia
(03) 517-2755

National Anti-Bias Task Force
c/o Anne Glover
University of South Australia
Lorne Avenue
Magill, South Australia 5072

Further Readings

CANADIAN

See Training Resources, above, for additional readings.

Ashworth, Mary
    1993. *Children of the Canadian Mosaic: A Brief History to 1950*. Toronto, ON:
    Ontario Institute for Studies in Education.

Bopp, Judie, Michael Bopp, Lee Brown, and Phil Lane
    1984. *The Sacred Tree*. Lethbridge, AB: Four Worlds Development Press.

Canadian Council of Ministers of Education
    1986. *Multicultural Education Policies in Canada*. Toronto, ON:
    Canadian Council of Ministers of Education.

Chud, Gyda, and Ruth Fahlman
    1985. *Early Childhood Education for a Multicultural Society: A Handbook for
    Educators*. Vancouver, BC: Pacific Education Press.

Coehlo, Elizabeth
    1988. *Caribbean Students in Canadian Schools*, Book 1. Toronto, ON: Carib-Can
    Publishers.

———.
    1993. *Caribbean Students in Canadian Schools*, Book 2. Markham, ON: Pippin
    Publishing.

Dickason, Olive
> 1992. *Canada's First Nations: A History of Founding Peoples from Earliest Times.* Markham, ON: Pippin Publishing.

Dotsch, Julie, and Jane McFarlane
> 1992. *The Newcomer Preschool: A Resource Book for Teachers.* Ottawa, ON: Ministry of Culture and Recreation.

Fleras, Augie, and Jean Elliott
> 1992. *Multiculturalism in Canada: The Challenge of Diversity.* Scarborough, ON: Nelson Canada.

Gouthro, Mary Beth
> 1992. "Exercising an Anti-Biased Curriculum in Nova Scotia Child Care." *Connections* 4, 3: 1.

Haegert, Dorothy
> 1989. *Children of the First People,* 2nd ed. Vancouver, BC: Arsenal Pulp Press.

Herberg, Dorothy
> 1993. *Frameworks for Cultural and Racial Diversity.* Toronto, ON: Canadian Scholar's Press.

James, Carl
> 1993. *Towards A New Response: Race Relations in Childcare Programs.* Toronto, ON: Municipality of Metropolitan Toronto.

Johnston, Basil
> 1979. *Ojibway Heritage.* Toronto, ON: McClelland & Stewart.

———.
> 1983. *Ojibway Ceremonies.* Toronto, ON: McClelland & Stewart.

Kehoe, John
> 1984. *A Handbook for Enhancing the Multicultural Climate of the School.* Vancouver, BC: Pacific Education Press, University of British Columbia.

Kerr, K., K. Wickens, and G. Wickens
> 1988. *Rainbow Feelings—A Conflict Resolution Handbook.* Burnaby, BC: Public Education for Peace Society.

Lee, Enid
> 1985. *Letters to Marcia: A Teacher's Guide to Anti-Racist Education.* Toronto, ON: Cross-Cultural Communication Centre.

McLeod, Keith, ed.
> 1984. *Multicultural Early Education.* Guidance Centre, Faculty of Education, University of Toronto. Toronto, ON: University of Toronto.

————.
1987. *Multicultural Education: A Partnership*. Ottawa, ON: Canadian Council for Multicultural and Intercultural Education.

Manitoba. Department of Employment Services and Economic Security.
1987. *One Child. Two Cultures*. Immigration and Settlement Branch. Winnipeg, MB: Department of Employment Services and Economic Security.

Meyers, Mary
1993. *Teaching to Diversity. Teaching and Learning in the Multi-Ethnic Classroom*. Toronto, ON: Irwin Publishing.

Mock, Karen
1986. *Multicultural Early Childhood Education in Canada*. Ottawa, ON: Multicultural Sector, Department of Secretary of State.

Mock, K., and V. Masemann
1987. *Multicultural Teacher Education in Canada*. Ottawa, ON: Multicultural Sector, Department of Secretary of State.

Morris, Sonia, ed.
1989. *Multicultural and Intercultural Education: Building Canada*. Ottawa, ON: Canadian Council for Multicultural and Intercultural Education.

Murphy Kilbride, Kenise
1990. *Multicultural Early Childhood Education—A Resource Kit*. Toronto, ON: Ryerson Polytechnic Institute.

National Commission on Aboriginal Childcare
1992. *Our Children Our Ways: An Exploration into Native Child Care Issues*. Ottawa, ON: Native Council of Canada.

Native Council of Canada
1990. *Native Child Care: The Circle of Care*. Ottawa, ON: Native Council of Canada.

1984–91. *New Friends: Alternatives to Racism*. Curriculum Series for K to Grade 5. Vancouver, BC: Pacific Education Press.

Salegio, Mary, and Bernice Pelletier
1991. *Atonement Home Multicultural Day Care Centre Manual and Resource Directory*. Edmonton, AB: The Franciscan Sisters Benevolent Society.

Schlesinger, R.A., and B. Schlesinger
1992. *Canadian Families in Transition*. Toronto, ON: Canadian Scholar's Press.

Slopin, Beverly, and Doris Seale
1992. *Through Indian Eyes: The Native Experience in Books for Young Children*. Gabriola Island, BC: New Society Publishers.

AMERICAN

The following represents a small selection of the extensive research and writings currently under way in the United States on the issues of diversity, multicultural education, and the anti-bias approach in early childhood programs.

Aboud, Frances
   1988. *Children and Prejudice*. New York: Basil Blackwell.

Berkeley, T.R., and B.L. Ludlow
   1989. "Toward a Reconceptualization of the Developmental Model." *Topics in Early Childhood Special Education* 9, 3: 51–66.

Cortes, C.E.
   1983. "Multiethnic and Global Education: Partners for the Eighties?" *Phi Beta Kappan* 64: 568–71.

Darder, A.
   1991. *Culture and Power in the Classroom: A Critical Foundation for Bicultural Education*. New York: Bergin and Garvey.

Derman-Sparks, L.
   1992. "Reaching Potentials through Antibias, Multicultural Curriculum." In *Reaching Potentials: Appropriate Curriculum and Assessment for Young Children*, Vol. 1, edited by S. Bredekamp and T. Rosegrant. Washington, DC: National Association for the Education of Young Children.

Derman-Sparks, L., and the A.B.C. Task Force
   1989. *The Anti-Bias Curriculum—Tools for Empowering Young Children*. Washington, DC: NAEYC.

Derman-Sparks, L., C.T. Higa, and B. Sparks.
   1980. "Children, Race and Racism: How Race Awareness Develops." *Interracial Books for Children Bulletin* 11: 3–9.

Doyle, A.B., J. Beaudet, and F.E. Aboud
   1988. "Developmental Patterns in the Flexibility of Children's Ethnic Attitudes." *Journal of Cross-Cultural Psychology* 19: 3–18.

Gonzalez-Mena, J.
   1993. *Multicultural Issues in Child Care*. Mountain View, CA: Mayfield Publishing.

Grant, C., and C. Sleeter
   1987. "An Analysis of Multicultural Education in the United States." *Harvard Educational Review* 57: 421–44.

Hinderlie, V., M. McCullough, M. Schachter, P. Simmons, and S. Wertis
   1978. *Caring for Children in a Social Context: Eliminating Racism, Sexism and Other Patterns of Discrimination*. Cambridge, MA: Multicultural Project.

Jipson, J.
1991. "Developmentally Appropriate Practice: Culture, Curriculum and Connections." *Early Education and Development* 2: 120–136.

Katz, P.A.
1982. "Development of Children's Racial Awareness and Intergroup Attitudes." In *Current Topics in Early Childhood Education*, edited by L.G. Katz. Norwood, NJ: Ablex.

Kendall, Frances
1983. *Diversity in the Classroom: A Multicultural Approach*. New York: Teachers College Press.

Kessler, S. and B.B. Swadener, eds.
1992. *Reconceptualizing the Early Childhood Curriculum*. New York: Teachers College Press.

Lynch, E.W., and M.J. Hanson, eds.
1992. *Developing Cross-Cultural Competence: A Guide for Working with Young Children and Their Families*. Baltimore, MD: Paul H. Brookes.

Mallory, B., and R. New, eds.
1994. *Diversity and Developmentally Appropriate Practices*. New York: Teachers College Press.

Matiella, Ana C.
1991. *Positively Different: Creating a Bias-Free Environment for Young Children*. Santa Cruz, CA: Network Publications.

Neugebauer, Bonnie, ed.
1992. *Alike and Different: Exploring Our Humanity with Young Children*. Washington, DC: NAEYC.

Ogbu, J.U.
1992. "Understanding Cultural Diversity and Learning." *Educational Researcher* 21, 8: 5–14.

Phillips, Carol
1988. "Nurturing Diversity for Today's Children and Tomorrow's Leaders." *Young Children* (January): 42–47.

Phillips, D., K. McCartney, S. Scarr, and C. Howes
1987. "Reflective Review of Infant Day Care Research: A Cause for Concern." *Zero to Three* 7, 3: 18–21.

Pusch, M.D., ed
1979. *Multicultural Education: A Cross-Cultural Training Approach*. Chicago, IL: Intercultural Network.

Ramsey, P.G.
    1986a. "Racial and Cultural Categories." In *Promoting Social and Moral Development in Young Children: Creative Approaches for the Classroom*, edited by C.P. Edwards. New York: Teachers College Press.

———.
    1986b. "Young Children's Thinking about Ethnic Differences." In *Children's Ethnic Socialization: Pluralism and Development*, edited by J. Phiney and M. Rotheran. Beverley Hills, CA: Sage.

———.
    1987. *Teaching and Learning in a Diverse World: Multicultural Education for Young Children*. New York: Teachers College Press.

Rogoff, B., M. Gouvain, and S. Ellis
    1984. "Development Viewed in Its Cultural Context." In *Developmental Psychology*, edited by Bornstein and Lamb. Hillsdale, NJ: Erlbaum.

Saracho, O., and B. Spodek
    1986. *Understanding the Multicultural Experience in Early Childhood Education*. Washington, DC: NAEYC.

———.
    1990. *Early Childhood Teacher Preparation in Cross-Cultural Perspectives*, Vol. 1. New York: Teachers College Press.

Spodek, B.
    1991. "Early Childhood Curriculum and Cultural Definitions of Knowledge." In *Yearbook in Early Childhood Education: Vol. 2. Issues in Early Childhood Curriculum*, edited by O. Saracho and B. Spodek. New York: Teachers College Press.

York, Stacey
    1991. *Roots and Wings. Affirming Culture in Early Childhood Programs*. St. Paul, MN: Redleaf Press.

Zimiles, H.
    1991. "Diversity and Change in Young Children: Some Educational Implications." In *Yearbook in Early Childhood Education*, Vol. 2., edited by O. Saracho and B. Spodek. New York: Teachers College Press.

INTERNATIONAL

Clarke, P., and J. Millikan
    1986. *Developing Multicultural Perspectives in Early Childhood*. Free Kindergarten Association. Richmond, Australia: Multicultural Resource Centre.

Commission for Racial Equity
    1990. *From Cradle to School: A Practical Guide to Race Equality and Child Care*. London: Commission for Racial Equality.

Donoghue, J.
1991. "Entitlement for All: Race, Gender, and ERA—A Perspective from the NCC." *Multicultural Teaching* 10, 1.

East, Helen
1991. *The Singing Sack: 28 Song-Stories from around the World*. London: A and C Black Publishing.

Epstein, D., and A. Sealey
1990. *Where It Really Matters: Developing Anti-Racist Education in Predominantly White Primary Schools*. Birmingham: Development Education Centre.

Gill, D., B. Mayor, and M. Blair, eds.
1992. *Racism and Education: Structures and Strategies*. London: Sage.

Hall, J., C. Porter, and P. Clarke
1989. *Incorporating a Multicultural Perspective Programme: Planning for Early Childhood*. Free Kindergarten Association. Richmond, Australia: Multicultural Resource Centre.

National Children's Bureau
1993. *Anti-Sexist Child Care Practice/Sex Role Stereotyping in Young Children*. London: National Children's Bureau.

Siraj-Blatchford, Iram
1994. *The Early Years. Laying the Foundations for Racial Equality*. Stoke-on-Trent: Trentham Books.

Troyna, B., and B. Carrington
1990. *Education, Racism and Reform*. London: Routledge.

Troyna, B., and R. Hatcher
1992. *Racism in Children's Lives*. London: Routledge and National Children's Bureau.

Yeatman, A.
1988. "A Review of Multicultural Policies and Programs in Children's Services." Canberra, Australia: Office of Multicultural Affairs.

Appendix

Glossary

References

Copyright Acknowledgments

Index

Happy New Year

Selamat Hari Natal
&
Tahun Baru

تام لوگوں کو نورسی اور نئے سال کی دلی مبارک باد

BUON CAPO D'ANNO!

BONU NOADDU ANNU!   YENI YILINIZ KUTLU OLSUN!

BONNE ET HEUREUSE ANNEE!   GELUKKIG NIEUW JAAR!   SRETNA NOVA GODINA!

BUONO CAPRILANO!   BLYTHEN MAD DA!   Щасливого Нового Року!

GLEDILEKT NYT AR!   BON PRINCIPI!   Saal Mubarak

GLAEDELIGT NYT AAR!   GLUECKLICHES NEUES JAHR!   FELIZ AÑO NUEVO!

এইচ - হতুন   GODT NYTTAAR!   BLIADHAN NUA FE MHAISE DHUIT!

EVTIKHES TO NEON ETOS!   Честито Ви Новата Година!

SALE NOW MOBARAK BAD!   TI AUGURI UN BIJON ANNO!   FELIZ ANO NOVO!

Шчасьливого Новага Году!   SWASDI BEPEE MA!   AFRENHYEA PA!

DAUDZ LAIMES JUANA GADA!   ISSENA IT TAIBA!   BOLDOG UIEVET KIVANUNK!

BLEIN VIE NOA!   BLWYDDYN NEWYDD DDA!   LAIMINGU NAUJU METU!

BLIADHNA MHATH UR!   A GLICKLUCH NIE YUOR!   С Новым Годом!

Сретна Нова Година!   MASAGAMANG BAGONG TAON!

ꨀꨯꨂꨁꩃ - ꨡꨯꨂ   新年快樂   CHÀO MÙNG NĂM MƠÍ

ꨀꩃꨀꨯ   새해 복 많이 받으세요   Χρόνια Πολλά

LANGUAGES	Mother	Father	Sister
FRENCH	la mère	le père	la soeur
CHINESE	母親 (妈妈) mā mā　mǔ qin	父親 (爸爸) bàbà　'fù qin	姐妹 vie mei
GERMAN	Mutter	Vater	Schwester
GREEK	Μητἐρα meetera	Ματἐρας pateras	àδελϬń adelfee
GUJARTI (INDIA)	ылા	બાપુજ	બહેન
HINDI	Mata Ji	Pita Ji	Bhen
ITALIAN	la madre la mamma	il padre il padre	la sorella la sorella
NORWEGIAN	Mor	Far	Søster
PORTUGUESE	Mãe	Pai	Irmã
TAGALOG (PHILIPPINES)	Ina	Ama	Ate
POLISH	Mama	Tata	Siostra
SPANISH	Mama'	Papa'	Hermana
VIETNAMESE	me / má	cha / ba	chi (older sister) em gai (younger sister)
TAMIL	அம்மா Amma	அப்பா Appa	அக்கா　தங்கை acca (older)　thangai (younger)
RUSSIAN	MaMa	nana papa	cectpa (sestra)
HINDI	मा Ma	पाप PaPa	बेहन Behen
ROMANIAN	MAMA	TATA	SORĂ
TURKISH	ANNE A'NEH	BABA BA'BA	KIZ KAROES KIZ'CAR'DESH
PERSIAN	مادر mādar	پدر Pedar	خواهر Xahar
JAPANESE	お母さん okaasan	お父さん otoosan	younger = 妹さん imootrasan older = お姉市さん oneesan

Brother	Child	Week of the Child
le frère	l'enfant	La semaine de l'enfant
FU弟 xiong di	孩儿, 子 xian háil	孩儿子的一周 hái zǐ de yi zhōu
Bruder	Kind	Woche des Kindes
ὀδελϕός adelfōs	Μαιδτ pethee	Εβδομάδα τόχ Παιδιόν evdomatha too pethiou
ગ્1ઈ	ગ્1ગ્ફ	ગ્1ગ્ફ ગો ગ્ગ્1ગ્1ગ્1
Bhai	Bacha	Bachè ka saptaha
il fratello	il bumbino (boy) la bambina (girl)	La settimana dei bambini
Bror	Barn	Barnets Uge
Irmão	Crianca	Semana da crianca
Kuya	Bata	Lingo ng mga bata
brat	dziecko	Tydzień dziecka
Hermano	Niño (a)	La semana de los ninos (as)
anh (older brother) em trai (younger brother)	trè em thiêú nhi	Tuân lê̂ thiêú nhi
ங1ங்1ங் 3ங் anna (older) thumbi (younger)	ங்1ங்1ங்1ங் sirupillai	ங1ங்1ங்1ங்1ங்1ங்1ங் Pillaiyin kilamai Nadhal
δρατ (brat)	ребёнок (rebyonok)	неделя детей
भाई Bhai	बच्चे Bachehé	बच्चों का सप्ताह Bachchon ka Saptah
FRATE	COPIL	SĂPTĂMÎNA COPILULUI
ERKEK KARDEŞ ER'CEK CAR'DESH	ϛocuk CHO'JUWK	HAFTANIN ϛOCUĞU HAFTA'NIN CHO'JUWU
برادر baradar	کودک Kūdak	هفته‌ی کودک Hapte-ye Kūdak
younger = 弟さん otootosan older = お兄さん oniisan	子供 Kodomo	子供の週間 kodomo no shuukan

LANGUAGES	Cherish the Children	Welcome	Good Morning
FRENCH	Cherissons les enfants	Bienvenue	Bonjour
CHINESE	珍惜孩子们 zhén xī húi zǐ mén	欢迎 huān yeng	早晨好 zǎo chén hǎo
GERMAN	Schätzt die Kinder	WillKommen	Guten Morgen
GREEK	να αγαπάτε τα πεδιά	Καλοσορίσατε Kalosoreesateh	Καλή μέρα kaleemera
GUJARTI (INDIA)	બાળક ને પ્રેમ કરો Balak ne prem Karo	ભલે પધારો Bhale Padharo	સુપ્રભાતમ (સુ પ્રભાત) Suprabhatham
HINDI	Bachaa ka utsah badao	Swagatam	Namaskar ←
ITALIAN	Amiamo i bambini	Benvenuti	Buon giorno
NORWEGIAN	Voerne om børnene	Velkommen	God morgen
PORTUGUESE	Couidado com amor	Benvindo	Bom dia
TAGALOG (PHILIPPINES)	Mahalin ang mga bata (LOVE THE CHILDREN)	Tuloy kayo (COME IN)	Magandang um aga
POLISH	Kochaé dziecko	Witam	dzień dobry
SPANISH	Cuidando los ninos (as) (TAKE CARE OF THE CHILDREN)	Bienvenido	Buenos Días
VIETNAMESE	yêu mêń trè em	chao mủng	chaó buỏi sáng
TAMIL	சிறுமிகளை நேசி Olrizmogzn		குழந்தைகளை நேசி Kallal Vanakkam
PERSIAN	عشق به کودکان ešɣ be Kudakan	خوش آمدید Xoš āmaclid	صبح به خیر sobh be-xeyr
ROMANIAN	ÎNGRIJITI COPIIII! (aprot.)	BUN VENIT!	BUNĂ DIMINEAȚA
RUSSIAN	utsakappaduthuthal Уважайте детей (Respect the children)	С приездом	Доброе утро
HINDI	बच्चों को उत्साह दें Bachchon Ko Utsah dé.	स्वागतम् Swagatam	नमस्कार Namaskar
TURKISH	ÇOCUKLARI SEVİNİZ CHO'J K'LARY SEV'IN'IS	HOS ÇELDINIZ HOSH GEL'DIN'IS	GÜNAYDIN GOON 'EYE' DIN
JAPANESE	子供をとてもかわいがってくれます。 kodomo wo totemo Kawainatte Kuremasu.	いらしゃいます irashaimase	お早うございます。 ohayoogozaimasu.

Good Afternoon	Good Evening	Hello	Thank You
Bon après-midi	Bonsoir	Salut	Merci
下午好 午安 xià wǔ hǎo	晚晚安 wǎn shang hǎo	喂你好 wèi	谢谢打下天 xiè nǐ
Guten Tag	Guten Abend	Hallo	Dankeschön
Καλη Μέρα (us hello) καλό απόγευμα (us goodbye)	καλη σπέρα	Τι κάνεις Tee Kanees	Ευχαριστό Efhareesto
어서갈니라	어서갈니라	후메에!	갈아이라
⟶	⟶	Kemcho	Aabhar
Buon pommeriggio	Buona sera	Ciao	Grazie
God dag	God aften	Hallo	Tak
Boa tarde	Boa noite	Olá	Obrigado
Magan dang hapon	Mogandang gabi	Hello	Salamat Po
⟶	dobry wieczur	Cześi	dziękuję
Buenas tardes	Buenas noches	Hola	Gracias
chaō buổi chieu	chaō buổi tối	chaō	
மாலை வணக்கம்	மாலை வணக்கம் Mallai Vanakkam	Hello	Nantri
عصر بخیر Asr be-xeyr	بعد الظهر بخیر ba'd-Azzohr bexeyr	سلام Salām	متشکرم motaš akker-am
BUNǍ ZIUA	BUNǍ SEARA	SALUT	MULTUMESC
	Добрый вечер	Здравствуйте	Спасибо
⟶	⟶	⟶	धन्यवाद or शुक्रिया Dhanyavad or Shookria
TÜNAYDIN TOON'EYE'DIN	İYİ AKŞAMLAR E'YEE UK'SH M'LAR	MERHABA MEH'RAH'BA	TEŞEKKÜREDERIM TESH'EK'KOOR' ED'ER'IM.
今日は. konnichi wa.	今晩は. konban wa.	今日は. konnichiwa.	どうも ありがとう ございます. domo arigato gozaimse.

GLOSSARY

Acceptance	The ability to honour a person or group for who they are, without any conditions attached
Anti-bias	An approach that actively challenges inequities in order to bring about change for the better
Awareness	The emergence of seeing and understanding new ideas and things
Bias	Any attitude or feeling that tends to favour or reject individuals or groups because of what they represent
Commission	Empowerment, carrying through
Critical thinking	The ability to look at statements and situations—at the positive and negative—before deciding whether to agree or disagree
Discrimination	Differentiation based on preset ideas about a group or a person resulting in nonacceptance of that group or person
Dismissal technique	The habit of ignoring or not paying attention to a comment
Divergent	Expanding, branching off into many different directions
Divergent question	A question phrased in such a way that there are many possible answers. Any answer is acceptable; there is no one correct answer. Inserting "How do you think ...?" will make any question a divergent one.
Diversity	Dissimilarities, differences, variety
Empathy	The ability to put oneself in another person's place and understand how that person feels without feeling pity for that person
Exposure	Continued experiences to and with new things and ideas
Facilitator	A person who provides opportunities/experiences in order to guide learning
Familiarity	The possession of a *little* bit of knowledge about new ideas and things
Homophobia	Fear of same-sex life style and anything associated with it

Inclusion	Admission into, or feeling a part of a group
Omission	Elimination, leaving out—either on purpose or by accident
Prejudice	A prejudgment of a person based not on facts but on suppositions; an attitude formed about a person or group without any real knowledge of that person or group
Pro-activism	The ability to take action and challenge injustice, to do something positive to bring about change for the better
Problem-solving	Thinking things through and arriving at possible solutions
Projectile management	The ability to throw an item into a designated spot
Racism	A feeling, opinion, attitude, or action on the part of individuals or institutions that denies a person or group equality because of their race (skin colour or facial features)
Respect	Listening to, without necessarily agreeing with, others' points of view in a nonthreatening, nonjudgmental atmosphere
Self-esteem	How a person feels about himself
Self-identity	How a person defines himself
Sense of agency	A feeling that one is the cause of an action, that one has made something happen
Stereotype	An overgeneralization and oversimplified idea about a particular person or group, either positive or negative
Tokenism	Providing only one of an item that is different (e.g., one First Nations doll among many white dolls); doing something that is different once only, such as eating Asian food on a day designated to celebrate Asian customs
Tolerate	To put up with, to endure ("tolerate" has negative connotations)
Value	An idea or concept that is very meaningful and worthwhile to an individual or a society

References

Aboud, F.
> 1988. *Children and Prejudice*. New York: Basil Blackwell.

Allen, J., E. McNeill, and V. Schmidt
> 1992. *Cultural Awareness for Children*. Menlo Park, CA: Addison-Wesley.

Biocchi, S., and S. Radcliffe
> 1983. *A Shared Experience: Bridging Cultures—Resources for Cross Cultural Training*. London, ON: London Cross Cultural Learning Centre.

Brazelton, T.B.
> 1974. *Toddlers and Parents*. New York: Delacourte Press.

Bredekamp, S., ed.
> *Developmentally Appropriate Practice in Early Childhood Programs Serving Children from Birth through Age 8*, exp. ed. Washington, DC: National Association for the Education of Young Children.

Bredekamp, S., and T. Rosegrant, eds.
> 1992. *Reaching Potentials: Appropriate Curriculum and Assessment for Young Children*, Vol. 1. Washington, DC: National Association for the Education of Young Childen.

Cassidy, D., and C. Lancaster
> 1993. "The Grassroots Curriculum: A Dialogue between Children and Teachers." *Young Children* 48, 6: 47–51.

Chud, G., and R. Fahlman
> 1985. *Early Childhood Education for a Multicultural Society: A Handbook for Educators*. Vancouver, BC: Pacific Education Press.

Derman-Sparks, L.
> 1992. "Reaching Potentials through Anti-Bias, Multicultural Curriculum." In *Reaching Potentials: Appropriate Curriculum and Assessment for Young Children*, Vol. 1, edited by S. Bredekamp and T. Rosegrant. Washington, DC. National Association for the Education of Young Children.

Derman-Sparks, L., and the A.B.C. Task Force
> 1989. *The Anti-Bias Curriculum: Tools for Empowering Young Children*. Washington, DC: National Association for the Education of Young Children.

Feeney, S., D. Christensen, and E. Moravcik
> 1991. *Who Am I in the Lives of Children*, 4th ed. New York: Merrill.

Fowell, N., and J. Lawton
> 1992. "An Alternative View of Appropriate Practice in E.C.E." *Early Childhood Research Quarterly* 7: 53–73.

Gonzalez-Mena, J.
   1993. *Multicultural Issues in Child Care*. Mountain View, CA: Mayfield Publishing.

Grunfield, F.
   1975. *Games of the World. How to Make Them. How to Play Them. How They Came to Be*. Zurich: Swiss Committee for UNICEF.

Hall, N.
   1993. "Linking Knowledge and Experience: A Model for Training Infant/Toddler Caregivers and Infant Mental Health Practitioners." *Zero to Three: National Centre for Clinical Infant Programs* 14, 1: 15–20.

Hall, N., and B. Flint
   1991. "Infant Curriculum: Training the Trainers." Presentation at Ontario College of Applied Arts and Technology Conference, Orillia, ON, May.

Hall, N., J. Thompson, and L. Day
   1993. *The Caring Circle: Train the Trainers Manual*. Toronto, ON: Canadian Mothercraft Society and Native Child and Family Services.

Hall, N., and V. Rhomberg
   1994. "Literacy and Families: An Anti-Bias Approach." *Canadian Association of Young Children* 19, 1.

Hass, G.
   1983. *Curriculum Planning: A New Approach*, 4th ed. Boston, MA: Allyn and Bacon.

Hunter, I., and M. Judson
   1977. *Simple Folk Instruments to Make and Play*. New York: Simon and Schuster.

James, C.
   1993. *Towards a New Response: Race Relations in Childcare Programs*. Toronto, ON: Municipality of Metropolitan Toronto.

Katz, L.
   1983. "What Is Basic for Young Children?" In *Curriculum Planning: A New Approach*, 4th ed., edited by G. Hass. Boston: Allyn and Bacon.

Kehl, M., and C. Gainer
   1991. *Good Earth Art: Environmental Art for Kids*. Bellingham: Bright Ring Publishing.

Kehoe, J.
   1984. *A Handbook for Enhancing the Multicultural Climate of the School*. Vancouver BC: Pacific Education Press, University of British Columbia.

Kehoe, J., and E. Mansfield
  1993. "The Limitations of Multicultural Education and Anti-Bias Education."
  Multiculturalism XV, Nos. 2/3: 4.

Labinowicz, E.
  1980. *The Piaget Primer*. Menlo Park, CA: Addison-Wesley.

McFarlane, C.
  1986. *Hidden Messages? Activities for Exploring Bias*. Birmingham, England:
  Development Education Centre.

Maguire, J.
  1990. *Hopscotch, Hangman, Hot Potato and HaHaHa. A Rulebook of Children's
  Games*. Englewood Cliffs, NJ: Prentice Hall.

Mallory, B., and R. New, eds.
  1994. *Diversity and Developmentally Appropriate Practices*. New York: Teachers
  College Press.

Matiella, A.C.
  1991. *Positively Different: Creating a Bias-Free Environment for Young Children*.
  Santa Cruz, CA: Network Publications.

Miller, D.F.
  1989. *First Steps toward Cultural Difference: Socialization in Infant/Toddler Day
  Care*. Washington, DC: Child Welfare League of America.

Mock, K.
  1988. *Race Relations Training: A Manual and Resource Guide for Practitioners and
  Consultants*. Race Relations Directorate. Toronto, ON: Ontario Ministry of
  Citizenship.

Murphy Kilbride, K.
  1990. *Multicultural Early Childhood Education Facilitator's Manual*. Toronto,
  ON: Ryerson Polytechnic Institute.

Neugbauer, B., ed.
  1992. *Alike and Different: Exploring Our Humanity with Young Children*.
  Washington, DC: National Association for the Education of Young Children.

New York Board of Education
  1988. *Promoting Bias-Free Curriculum Materials: A Resource Guide for Staff
  Development*. New York: Board of Education.

Ontario Women's Directorate
  1993. *Words That Count Women Out/In*. Toronto, ON: Ontario Women's
  Directorate.

Parks, S.
  1986. *Make Every Step Count. Birth to One Year*. Palo Alto, CA: VORT Corp.

Petrash, C.
  1992. *Simple Environmental Activities for Young Children*. Mt. Rainer, MD: Gryphon House.

Phillips, D., K. McCartney, S. Carr, and C. Howes
  1987. "Reflective Review of Infant Day Care Research: A Cause for Concern." *Zero to Three* 7, 3: 18–21.

Pollution Probe
  1991. *Canadian Green Calendar*. Toronto, ON: McClelland & Stewart.

Ramsey, P.
  1987. *Teaching and Learning in a Diverse World: Multicultural Education for Young Children*. New York: Teachers College Press.

Raths, L., M. Harmin, and S. Simon
  1978. *Values and Teaching: Working with Values in the Classroom*, 2nd ed. Columbus, OH: Merrill Publishing.

Raths, L., S. Wassermann, A. Jonas, and A. Rothstein
  1986. *Teaching for Thinking: Theory, Strategies and Activities for the Classroom*, 2nd ed. New York: Teachers College Press.

Recycling Council of Ontario and Metropolitan Toronto Works Department
  1992. *Be Good to Your Garden Compost!* Toronto, ON.

Rhomberg, V.
  1993. "Anti-Bias: A Curriculum beyond Multiculturalism." Paper presented at the Canadian Child Care Federation National Conference, Toronto, ON, May.

————.
  1993–94. *The E.C.E. Exchange*, Association of Early Childhood Educators, Toronto Branch (Ontario) Newletter: "Anti-Bias—What Does It Mean?" (winter 1993); "Anti-Bias—Barriers: Resources" (spring 1993); "Anti-Bias—Resources: Books, Items, Equipment—Appropriateness and Sources" (summer 1993); "Anti-Bias—Holidays and Celebrations" (fall 1993); "Anti-Bias and the Family" (winter 1994); "Anti-Bias—Steps Leading to Understanding of Respect for Each Family" (spring 1994); "Anti-Bias—Affirming All Families" (fall 1994).

————.
  1993–94. *The E.C.E. Link*, Association of Early Childhood Educators Provincial Newsletter: (a) "The Anti-Bias Approach in Early Childhood Education: An Introduction" (winter 1993); (b) "The Anti-Bias Approach: Barriers towards Implementation" (spring 1993); (c) "The Anti-Bias Approach: Investigation of Barriers (Training and Resources)" (summer 1993); (d) "Anti-Bias: Forming Meaningful Relationships with Families" (winter 1994); (e) "Anti-Bias: Strengthening Relationships with Families" (spring

1994); (f) "Anti-Bias: Sexuality and Families" (summer 1994); (g) "Anti-Bias: Maintaining Meaningful Relationships with Families" (fall 1994).

Simon, S., L. Howe, and H. Kirschenbaum
1972. *Values Clarification*. New York: Hart Publishing.

Stonehouse, A.
1990. "One Perspective on Programming for Toddlers." In *Trusting Toddlers: Planning for One- to Three-Year-Olds in Child Care Centers*, edited by Anne Stonehouse. St. Paul, MN: Toys 'n Things Press.

Stonehouse, A., ed.
1990. *Trusting Toddlers: Planning for One- to Three-Year-Olds in Child Care Centers*. St. Paul, MN: Toys 'n Things.

Thompson, B.
1993. *Words Can Hurt You: Beginning a Program of Anti-Bias Education*. Menlo Park, CA: Addison-Wesley.

Toronto Board of Education
1991. *Anti-Racist Education and the Adult Learner*. Toronto, ON: Toronto Board of Education: Continuing Education Department.

Vulpe, S.
1977. *Vulpe Assessment Battery*, 2nd ed. Toronto, ON: National Institute on Mental Retardation.

Williams, L.
1991. "Curriculum Making in Two Voices: Dilemmas of Inclusion in Early Childhood Education." *Early Childhood Research Quarterly* 6: 303–11.

York, S.
1992. *Developing Roots and Wings. A Trainer's Guide to Affirming Culture in Early Childhood Programs*. St. Paul, MN: Redleaf Press.

Copyright Acknowledgments

Index

Notes

Notes

Notes

Notes

Notes

Notes

Notes

Notes

To the owner of this book

We hope that you have enjoyed *The Affective Curriculum*, and we would like to know as much about your experiences with this text as you would care to offer. Only through your comments and those of others can we learn how to make this a better text for future readers.

School _____ Your instructor's name _____

Course _____ Was the text required? _____ Recommended? _____

1. What did you like the most about *The Affective Curriculum?*

_____
_____
_____

2. How useful was this text for your course?

_____
_____
_____

3. Do you have any recommendations for ways to improve the next edition of this text?

_____
_____
_____

4. In the space below or in a separate letter, please write any other comments you have about the book. (For example, please feel free to comment on reading level, writing style, terminology, design features, and learning aids.)

_____
_____
_____

Optional
Your name _____ Date _____

May Nelson Canada quote you, either in promotion for *The Affective Curriculum* or in future publishing ventures?

Yes _____   No _____

Thanks!

AIL ⇒ POSTE

Corporation / Société canadienne des postes

ge paid   Port payé
Canada   si posté au Canada

ess   Réponse
                 d'affaires

0107077099   01

0107077099-M1K5G4-BR01

Nelson Canada
College Editorial Department
1120 Birchmount Rd.
Scarborough, ON M1K 9Z9

PLEASE TAPE SHUT. DO NOT STAPLE.